Multiculturalism

Multiculturalism

A Shalom Motif for the Christian Community

CHINAKA SAMUEL DOMNWACHUKWU
and HEEKAP LEE

WIPF & STOCK · Eugene, Oregon

MULTICULTURALISM
A Shalom Motif for the Christian Community

Copyright © 2014 Chinaka Samuel DomNwachukwu and Heekap Lee. All rights reserved. Except for brief quotations in critical publications or reviews, no part of this book may be reproduced in any manner without prior written permission from the publisher. Write: Permissions. Wipf and Stock Publishers, 199 W. 8th Ave., Suite 3, Eugene, OR 97401.

Unless otherwise noted, all Scripture quotations are taken from the Holy Bible, New International Version®, NIV®. Copyright © 1973, 1978, 1984, 2011. Used by permission of Zondervan. All rights reserved worldwide. www.zondervan.com

Scripture quotations marked kjv are taken from the King James Version.

Wipf & Stock
An Imprint of Wipf and Stock Publishers
199 W. 8th Ave., Suite 3
Eugene, OR 97401

www.wipfandstock.com

ISBN 13: 978-1-62032-991-7

Manufactured in the U.S.A.

Contents

List of Figures and Tables   vi
Preface   vii
Acknowledgments   ix

1. The Prevailing Philosophies and Ideologies that Inform Contemporary Christian Worldviews Today   1
2. Contemporary Thought on the Christian Worldview and the Implications for Multiculturalism   16
3. The Facts and Fallacies of the Christian Views on Multiculturalism   34
4. The Goals of Multicultural Education   50
5. Justice: A Central Idea in Multiculturalism   57
6. Biblical Foundations for Multiculturalism   66
7. Shalom: A New Paradigm for Multiculturalism   96
8. Shalom: A Kingdom Motif for the Educational Setting   112
9. Multicultural Stories: Exemplars for Life in a Shalom Community   121
10. Shalom: A Kingdom Motif for the Twenty-first-Century Church   128
11. Taking the Steps Towards a Multicultural Community   136

Bibliography   141
Index   149

Figures

Figure 1.1   Gallup Poll of Party Leanings   13
Figure 6.1   Burnett's Human Characteristics   69
Figure 6.2   The Making of God's People   74
Figure 7.1   The Shalom Community Model   99
Figure 7.2   Three Dimensions of Cultural Identity   103

Tables

Table 3.1   Historical Enlightenment Paradigm   37
Table 3.2   Marxist and Postmodern Educators   40
Table 7.1   Two Approaches to Multiculturalism   96
Table 7.2   Stages of Multicultural Growth   105

Preface

THIS BOOK IS WRITTEN primarily for Christian churches and Christian educational communities. *Multiculturalism: A Shalom Motif for the Christian Community* is an attempt to engage the Christian community in the ongoing discussion of cultural diversity and its implications for the church of the twenty-first century. While some Christian scholars and church leaders have become intentional in their engagement of this all-important topic and its implication for the church in North America, others seem to take a hands-off approach to this topic, even working hard to distance themselves from any conversation on the topic.

An inescapable truth, however, is the fact that for the Christian church in North America to remain vibrant and relevant in the twenty-first century, it must engage with the idea of multiculturalism and all other forms of diversity that now characterize contemporary society. While the nature of the engagement will vary from case to case, cultural diversity has become a growing aspect of the church in America.

This book begins by engaging the extent to which political ideologies and party affiliations have influenced Christian responses to this concept of multiculturalism. It then addresses some of the contemporary Christian positions on multiculturalism, exposing the strengths and weaknesses of the arguments for and against multiculturalism in the Christian setting. A chapter is devoted to engaging the facts and fallacies of the Christian views on multiculturalism before making a case for the desired goals of multicultural education in schools and the implications those goals bear for the Christian community.

The biblical idea of social justice plays a prominent role in building a case for the biblical authenticity of multiculturalism. Social justice appears as a central idea in multiculturalism that is biblically based, and these biblical bases include the ideas of *imago Dei* (created in God's image), the

Preface

covenant relationship between God and humanity, *missio Dei* (the mission of God), *koinonia* (fellowship of God's people), and the biblical concept of God's kingdom. The book goes further to make a case for a shalom motif as a multicultural model for the Christian church and educational communities.

The book concludes with multicultural stories of real events within Christian communities in the United States, a discussion of shalom as a kingdom motif for the twenty-first century church, and suggested steps towards building a multicultural Christian community.

The two authors of this book have been on their own personal journeys towards the making of God's people. From his encounter with John Wilson Wallace to being a catalyst in the formation of a multicultural church in Pasadena, California, in the late 1990s, to more than a decade of teaching cultural diversity in the university, to extensive writings on multiculturalism, Chinaka brings a personal touch to this call for a shalom community. These are not just ideas, ideals, and dreams; rather, they represent what is possible within the community of faith when God's people allow themselves to be transformed through the renewing of their minds (Romans 12:1–2). Heekap was an eyewitness to the event involving Won-Joon Yoon, which is discussed in chapter 9, an event that transformed his life and sent him on a mission to call God's people to unity through his own teaching and preaching ministry.

It is our prayer that in reading this book, God's people will be able to take the focus away from the self and seek to make the kingdoms of this world the kingdom of our God and his Christ (Rev 11:15).

Acknowledgments

MANY PEOPLE HAVE CONTRIBUTED in no small measures to the success of this book project. Dr. Andre Robinson-Neal, a colleague at Azusa Pacific University, was the first to read through the manuscript and provided very constructive editorial feedback that shaped the structure of this book. Dr. Kenneth Waters, professor of biblical studies at Azusa Pacific University, provided critical theological feedback, while Dr. Jennifer Walsh, professor of political science, provided critical political contributions.

1

The Prevailing Philosophies and Ideologies that Inform Contemporary Christian Worldviews Today

MULTICULTURALISM IS AN IDEA, a dynamic movement, and a reality that the contemporary American Christian community must not only come to terms with, but must embrace for her to remain relevant for twenty-first century society. This embrace does not necessarily mean compromise, rather a deliberate effort to understand and constructively engage the changing dynamics of our twenty-first century society so as to continue being light to the darkness of this world and salt to its decay and rottenness. Multiculturalism has been identified by some within American evangelical Christian communities as a secular humanistic endeavor, which stems from Marxism and related concepts.[1] For this reason, multiculturalism as an idea has not enjoyed much reception within Christian communities, whether in academic circles or practical settings like churches and fellowships. The fact that some of the main philosophies and ideologies that have historically stood in opposition to the Christian worldview may be the precursors of this ideology have tended to disenfranchise Christians from any meaningful engagement with it.

> *The America way of life assumes that "All men are created equal . . ."*

---

1. Colson and Pearcey, *How Now Shall We Live?*

Multiculturalism

We live in an age and a time when Christianity is confronted by a growing opposition from secular humanistic worldviews and other opposing worldviews, which has led the church to become defensive in the face of new and pragmatic thoughts and ideologies such as multiculturalism. Noebel and Edwards present a number of these opposing ideologies and worldviews as Secular Humanism, Marxism-Leninism, and Cosmic Humanism. They argue that these philosophies consist of New Age pantheism and neo-paganism.[2] In order to meaningfully engage the idea of multiculturalism, we must define and understand these three ideologies and see them as the forces that have provided the basis for the arguments that have shaped Christian responses to multiculturalism. We must also explore some political ideologies that may play roles in making multiculturalism unappealing to some people within the evangelical community.

SECULAR HUMANISM

Humanism is a school of philosophy that presupposes that human beings rule their own destiny. This worldview is largely to blame for the contemporary spiritual chaos and purposeful departure from God, which currently characterizes many Western societies. It often assumes the nonexistence of God and underlies many anti-Christian philosophies and theories like the death of God theology, the theory of a distant and uninvolved God, and other forms of reasoning that remove the idea of God from people's everyday reality. To the secular humanistic mindset God is either dead or nonexistent or he is far removed from the earth and detached from whatever we do with our lives, leaving us the masters of our destinies.

The history of humanism can be traced back to a Greek philosopher of the fifth century named Protagoras, who proposed that man is the measure of all existence. His teachings can be summarized in words from his treatise *On the Gods*. Protagoras claimed that

> [i]n respect to the gods, I am unable to know either that they are or that they are not, for there are many obstacles to such knowledge, above all the obscurity of the matter, and the life of man, in that it is so short.[3]

---

2. Noebel and Edwards, *Thinking Like a Christian*.
3. Gomperz, *Greek Thinkers*, 448.

The Prevailing Philosophies and Ideologies

He went on, however, to deny the existence of any absolutes, asserting that humankind, "is the measure of all things," of things that are, that they are, and of things that are not, that they are not.[4] As far as Protagoras was concerned, nothing exists outside of the scope of human discovery and knowledge. It is ironic that humans attempted to nullify faith in a personal, immutable, and eternal God who transcends this universe on the basis of human knowledge.

This trend in philosophy enjoyed a progressive development until the seventeenth century when a combination of factors in science, philosophy, and theology gave it a great boost. Galileo Galilei had just given the world the thermometer, developed the pendulum, and applied the telescope to the study of the heavens. He had come on the heels of unpopular Copernicus, who had challenged the traditional theory that the world was the center of the universe and the sun revolved around the earth. As much as Galileo added credibility to Copernicus against the fury of the ecclesiastical orders Isaac Newton's theory of gravity emerged to give it an almost infallible credibility.

This apparent victory of physical science over traditional dogma was soon translated into an affront on all traditional theories, even religious theories. A prevailing idea of this era was that Galileo and his contemporaries did not only destroy the old universe, they unseated the old religions, traditional sciences, and philosophical theories that predated them.[5]

As this new age emerged, human reason became the final court of appeal in all matters of science, philosophy, and even religion. Just as Protagoras suggested, human beings became the measure of all things. Humanistic philosophers and practicing humanists often see Christians as uneducated and uninformed, narrow-minded and bigoted, superstitious and unsophisticated, and some have called them weak-minded. R. C. Sproul sums it up: modern humanism is anti-Christian. He substantiates his claim with the following reasons:

- In the nineteenth century, humanism saw religion not as a valid experience, but nevertheless a valuable experience since it calls humans to a higher level of virtue.

- Modern humanism tends to be more militant in its affront against Christianity.

---

4. Ibid., 461.
5. Cf. Schneider, "Introduction" to to *The Enlightenment*.

3

Multiculturalism

- Three important humanist publications—*A Humanist Manifesto* (1933), *Humanist Manifesto II* (1973), and *The Secular Humanist Declaration* (1980)—all affirm key aspects of humanism, some of which stand in opposition to the Christian faith:
  > The natural world is the only one we can know; the here-and-now is all there is.
  > Insight, intuition, and divine revelation must be tested by reason; truth is best discovered rationally.
  > Mankind is the only source of morals and values, and the highest human achievement is to improve the human condition.
- Since the nineteenth century, humanistic philosophers have accused Christianity of hindering the evolutionary progress of human beings by keeping people tied to the conservative outdated and antiquated frame of mind and values.[6]

Sproul accuses secular humanists of borrowing Christian ethical principles and ripping them off their Christian values. He accuses them of living on "borrowed capital." He sees modern humanism as basically atheistic, arguing that its nonatheistic forms can be found in the Unitarian Church. In its nonorganized forms, many church people have embraced its principles without knowing that they are humanistic.

Secular humanism has had a deleterious effect on the imperative of multiculturalism within Christian community, primarily because one argument suggests that humanist elements are present within the tenets of multiculturalism. However, multiculturalism is not humanistic in its true sense, primarily because, in its appeal to the dignity of the person and his/her rights, it does not make humans the measure of all things. Moreover, earliest Christian tradition affirmed multiculturalism as the will of God (cf. Acts 2:5–13; Gal 3:28; Eph 2:11–22; Rev 7:9).

POLITICAL IDEOLOGIES: A POWERFUL CHALLENGE TO AMERICAN CHRISTIANITY

The polarization of the American political landscape has created major challenges for multiculturalism, as some Christians see it as a liberal agenda opposed to their conservative Christian values. Many Americans

---

6. Sproul, *Lifeviews*.

have come to believe they must subscribe to one political ideology or the other. You are either Republican or Democrat, liberal or conservative. The landscape does not seem to provide much latitude for moderates from both sides. This pressure towards political leaning has rendered many churches and Christians incompetent in responding to the moral, social, and ideological contradictions that come with allegiance to a political ideology or party. This position overlooks the prospects and liabilities the church faces as it attempts to live her life as a stranger in this world (cf. 1 Pet 1:1–2). In order to adequately discuss the risks of these social and political labels as a defining identification for God's people, we will examine each label, what it stands for, and carefully critique its implications for God's people in addition to its implications for multiculturalism.

The hallmark of American democracy is a national endorsement of certain values, which make the American experience exceptional. These values include

- the worth and dignity of the individual;
- equality of all human beings;
- inalienable rights to life, liberty, property, and the pursuit of happiness;
- rights to freedom of speech, the press, religion, assembly, and private association;
- consent of the governed;
- majority rule;
- rule of law;
- due process of law;
- community and national welfare.[7]

These shared values unify Americans of all faiths, political convictions, as well as ethnicities and national origins. Sadly, however, this nation has recently developed a growing polarization that seems to overlook these areas of shared values but focuses exclusively on very small areas of differences defined by political leanings.

Whenever you see a definition of conservatism, the definition tends to ascribe to itself certain values that it assumes are absent in the liberal ideologies. Such values include "belief in personal responsibility, limited

---

7. Cf. Riseberg, "Framework and Foundations"; Kopellman and Goodhart, *Understanding Human Differences*, 4–5.

government, free market, individual liberty, traditional American values and a strong national defense."[8] An article titled "Conservative vs. Liberal Beliefs" contrasts conservatives and liberals, defining liberals as those who "believe in government action to achieve equal opportunity and equality for all. It is the duty of government to alleviate social ills and to protect civil liberties and individual and human rights."[9] Using these two definitions, let's ask some basic questions:

- When conservatives claim a belief in personal responsibility, do they truly believe that all liberals completely and outright dismiss personal responsibility in all circumstances?
- When conservatives claim belief in the free market and individual liberty, do they suggest that liberals (all liberals) hate the free market and individual liberty?

In the same spirit,

- When liberals are said to believe in government action to achieve equal opportunity and equality for all, does it mean that conservatives do not believe that the government has a role to play in ensuring equal opportunity and equality for all?
- When it is said that liberals believe it is the duty of government to alleviate social ills and protect civil liberties and individual and human rights, do the conservatives not share the same view? Do they truly advocate a survival of the fittest ideology even in the area of human rights and individual liberties, which they already made a paramount value for conservatism?

Since most evangelical Christians and many Roman Catholics tend to describe themselves as conservatives, let's take a moment and analyze what it means to be a "conservative," and then go further to contrast that with what it means to be a "liberal."

Who Is a Conservative?

Contrary to what many may think, there is no single definition for a conservative. There appears to be at least six kinds of conservatives: Cultural Conservatives, Crunchy Conservatives, Fiscal Conservatives, Neoconservatives,

8. "Conservative vs. Liberal Beliefs."
9. Ibid.

The Prevailing Philosophies and Ideologies

Social Conservatives, and Paleoconservative.[10] Let's attempt to define each brand of conservatism.

Cultural Conservatives. A common language used for cultural conservatives is that they hold onto traditional American values and ways of life, desiring to preserve them even amidst monumental cultural changes and diversity among them. It is an appeal to the "Good Old Days," which may not have been good for everyone, but certainly good for some. Those on the liberal end see it as backward leaning, rather than forward leaning. A large population of those who appeal to this orientation look back to the prominent Anglo-Saxon culture that dominated the America of yester year, without much regard to the American subcultures including the African American, Hispanic, and Native American heritage and values that all contributed to the amalgam now called the United States. Some who advocate a return to the traditional values fail to note that those values included slavery and slave holding, marginalization of women to the rank of personal property, and a grossly unequal society with extreme disregard for the individual liberties and rights of some Americans. While evangelical Christians and Roman Catholics tend to subscribe to this position, they often forget that the "Good Old Days" included gross intolerance against a variety of God's people: Baptists, Quakers, Jews, Mormons, and even Roman Catholics. While the "Good Old Days" may have been rooted in strong religiosity, it is doubtful that the spirituality of those days was better than today; otherwise, the revivals of George Whitefield and Jonathan Edwards would have been unnecessary.

Crunchy Conservatives. The emergence of "Crunchy Conservatives" is linked to the 2006 publication of the book *Crunchy Cons,* by Rod Dreher. This book raised awareness of a new breed of conservatives who go beyond the traditional conservative ideologies to distinguish themselves through a "decidedly un-materialistic and family-oriented" lifestyle. According to Quinn, in his analysis of Dreher, the Crunchy Cons "patronize small business such as organic food stores and markets, and recycle as if the world depended on it." Quinn went further in describing them: "Faith and religious duty are meshed, but there is a pronounced emphasis on not being preachy."[11]

Fiscal Conservatives. Fiscal conservatives have manifested their agenda to the American people recently through the Tea Party revolution. These

---

10. Quinn, "What Are the Different Types of Conservatives?"
11. Ibid.

individuals can be described as subscribing to small government (or even no government). They advocate little or no taxation, free market, reduction of government spending, reduction or even eradication of any government-sponsored social welfare system. Fiscal conservatives believe that individuals should be the ones making all the decisions about their money without governmental intrusion. Even though Ronald Reagan raised taxes during his time in office, most contemporary fiscal cons tend to view him as their model of fiscal conservatism. Fiscal conservatives are often referred to as economic conservatives or Libertarians. This is the block that supported Congressman Ron Paul in his 2012 political bid.

Neoconservatives. Neoconservatives are described as a countercultural movement that arose in the 1960s in reaction to government efforts to eradicate poverty, crime, and racial inequalities. Irving Kristol has been identified as the intellectual father of this ideology. He established this ideology through his critique of the welfare state and liberal social science.[12] According to Quinn, three things distinguish the Neocons: cutting tax rates and balancing the budget, enforcing morality and creating a more civil society, and aggressive nation building with the exportation of democracy as a fundamental foreign policy.

Social Conservatives. These conservatives tend to adopt a hard-line stance on many social issues of the day. They advocate a pro-life agenda, uphold abortion bans, and preach reduction of unwanted pregnancies. They adopt anti-gay positions and a definition of marriage as a union between one man and one woman. They believe in strong national defense, curtailing illegal immigration, protection of the American's right to bear arms (Second Amendment rights), and the restoration of prayer in schools, among many other social issues.

Paleoconservatives. Quinn defines this group as an "anticommunist and anti-globalization right wing movement, which emphasizes tradition, civil society and classical federalism, along with familial, religious, national and western identity."[13] This appears to be the perspective shared by many who supported Ron Paul, except that Paul's supporters also advocated fiscal conservatism and gun rights.

While some conservatives could comfortably subscribe to all of these six positions, it would be wrong to assume that most would. This means that even within the conservative circles diversity abounds.

12. "Irving Kristol."
13. Quinn," What are the Different Types of Conservatives?"

The Prevailing Philosophies and Ideologies

Conservatism as described above is slightly different from what Peter Berkowitz has termed constitutional conservatism. According to him, "constitutional conservatism puts liberty first and teaches the indispensableness of moderation in securing, preserving, and extending its blessings."[14] According to Berkowitz, the United States Constitution presupposes natural freedom and equality for all citizens. It draws legitimacy from democratic consent at the same time that it protects individual rights from "popular majorities."[15] Berkowitz concedes that individual freedom and individual responsibility, along with limited but energetic government where economic opportunities and strong national defense exist, capture the spirit of the Constitution while deriving its philosophical support from Edmund Burke, Adam Smith, John Stuart Mill, and Alexis de Tocqueville. Berkowitz, while praising the idea of constitutional conservatism, warns conservatives of two important facts:

1. The era of big government is here to stay because the vast majority of American people want it to stay.

2. The effects of the sexual revolution are here to stay. According to him, the invention of cheap and effective birth control and its wide and popular dissemination means that people can have sex more frequently without conceiving a child, quality of life is significantly enhanced—and the tide cannot be turned back.[16]

A summary of American conservatism can be stated as follows: Conservatives are those who favor less government involvement with regard to economic activity (so they generally prefer lower tax rates, less regulation) and more activity when it comes to preserving traditional social and religious freedom. It is erroneous to describe conservatives as being opposed to all government regulation, as even the staunchest conservatives want the government to prevent monopolies and enforce basic contractual arrangements. (Most conservatives also favor government policies to curb negative externalities, such as pollution of air and water, but this support varies with regard to the degree of intervention.) Conservatives would also prefer that community-level programs curb poverty rather than doing so with direct government aid, and religious conservatives would favor church-based solutions that would partner ministry with poverty relief.

14. Berkowitz, "Constitutional Conservatism," 3–23.
15. Ibid., 1.
16. Ibid., 15–16.

Typically, conservatives also favor the preservation of the nuclear family, restrictions on abortion, limits on access to pornography, and use of social control measures to curb drug use and crime. In most cases, conservatives are also in favor of strong defense policies and international agreements that aggressively promote American interests abroad.

Another political school of thought, similar to conservatism, the Libertarians, favors less government involvement with regard to economic activity and social issues. Thus, they are also likely to favor lower taxation and fewer government regulations, but also want less government interference on matters of personal liberty. Libertarians differ from conservatives in that they are often isolationist, preferring not to get involved in foreign disputes, and less supportive of social control measures at home. Therefore, they often support legalization of drugs, access to abortion, homosexual marriage, unimpeded access to pornography, and so forth—many issues that true conservatives would frown on.

With regard to traditional civil rights and liberties, conservatives and libertarians both support gun rights, free speech rights (except for obscene speech), and equal opportunity (which means opposing discrimination against racial and ethnic minorities and women, but not supporting affirmative action). Conservatives are more active champions of religious freedom, and they often advocate for the rights of religious groups to participate without restriction in the public square. Practically speaking, conservatives are in favor of using tax dollars to subsidize private schools and to allow college students to use government grants and subsidies at religious institutions. Libertarians on average are less concerned with religious freedom, although they support individual rights to worship (or not worship) without undue government interference.

A fundamental problem with the marriage between the Christian faith and conservatism lies in the progressive danger of conservative ideas comingling with Republican politics without an objective evaluation of the alignment or lack thereof of the political ideology with the conservative principles.[17] There is more danger when the church sides with this ideology without an objective critique of its principles.

17. Garry, "A Turning Point for Modern Conservatism."

Who Is a Liberal?

Irving Kristol, renowned American journalist and writer, is quoted as saying that a liberal is someone who "thinks it is all right for an 18-year-old girl to perform in a porn film so long as she is paid the minimum wage."[18] This caricature of liberalism is no surprise from a man who has come to be known as the intellectual father of neoconservatism. While the view reflected here would represent the view shared by some within the liberal wing of the American political spectrum, it is not representative of the views shared by all who take up that label. McClay presents a more representative and more intellectual definition of liberalism. According to him, liberalism is

> a doctrine upholding the independence and supreme value of the individual person as a free agent who bears fundamental rights that exist prior to and independently of government. . . . it regards the ultimate source of authority for all legitimate forms of government as the consent of the governed, as expressed in and through representative institutions.[19]

McClay went further to identify the unique elements that make up liberalism: a high degree of social tolerance, religious disestablishment, pluralism, and individualism. He links liberalism to the philosophical foundations established by John Locke and John Stuart Mill. He argues that liberalism echoes an idea made famous by Isaiah Berlin, who saw it as "a form of liberty that seeks above all else to protect the individual from coercion and to minimize the incursion of others into the zone of individual privacy."[20]

In his response to McClay's article, Yuval Levin confronts two kinds of liberalism. The first he described as progressivism. This, he argues, fits very well with the definition that McClay presented in his essay. He points out a second that he calls an "alternative to progressivism." He argues that this second kind finds voice in the works of Edmund Burke and Alexis de Tocqueville, in the wisdom of Publius, and "in the forms of the constitution that the authors of the *Federalist Papers* helped to design."[21] While he sees the first type of liberalism as the pursuit of an ideal society, he sees the second as the product of "countless generations of gradual political

---

18. Ibid.
19. McClay, "Liberalism after Liberalism," 26.
20. Ibid.
21. Levin, "Responses to Wilfred McClay," 33.

and cultural evolution in the West."²² The reality regarding liberalism in America is that a divergent stream of liberalism ranges from a blend of conservative and liberal ideals and ideas to extreme progressive thinking with absolute disregard to traditional values and institutions.

Liberals can also be divided into the two camps of liberals (or progressives) and populists. Progressives favor more government involvement in economic activity (and, thus, would be in favor of more government regulation and government-sponsored programs—and would support higher tax rates to pay for them), but they favor less government involvement in matters of personal liberty or personal conscience. Consequently, they often support policies such as homosexual marriage, unrestricted abortion, and less punishment (or legalization) for certain narcotic use. However, they do support government restrictions on firearm use, some restrictions on expressions of religion in the public square, and are in favor of rehabilitation approaches to crime and justice concerns. In the area of international affairs, liberals currently favor diplomacy over military action and are not averse to curbing American interests for the sake of global affairs.²³

With regard to civil rights and liberties, liberals are interested in policies that promote equality of results—not just equality of opportunity. They are also in favor of tax policies that shield the lower income groups from taxes, while increasing the tax rates for those in the upper income brackets. (The United States has this type of tax system already.) Liberals are also in favor of affirmative action programs and/or quota systems.

Populists are the opposite of Libertarians. They favor more government involvement in economic affairs (e.g., more government regulation, more government-sponsored social welfare programs), and more government intervention in social affairs. This means that they are more likely to support social control measures to curb promiscuity, pornography, and drug use. Populist policies often appeal to patriotic influences, and they are typically pro-military and pro-American interests when it comes to foreign affairs.

---

22. Ibid.

23. This is a recent policy change, since before Vietnam liberals were just as likely as conservatives to favor military invention and policies that curbed communist aggression.

WHAT IMPLICATIONS DO THESE LABELS BEAR FOR THE CHRISTIAN WITNESS?

A Baptist preacher was asked whether he was liberal or conservative, and his response was that he was liberal with his money and conservative with his wife. Political critics tend to argue that about 20 percent of Americans identify themselves as liberal; about 35 percent identify as conservatives, and approximately 40 percent describe themselves as moderates, indicating that a significant percentage of Americans do not fit the conservative or liberal labels. This figure differs greatly from the Gallup figures of 47 percent Democratic and 42 percent Republican in 2012. Pollsters use the language "Republican leaning" or "Democratic leaning" to produce higher figures to show U.S. party affiliations. The Gallup organization, for example, showed a significantly higher party affiliation/leanings in 2012 compared to what critics claim is a realistic representation.[24]

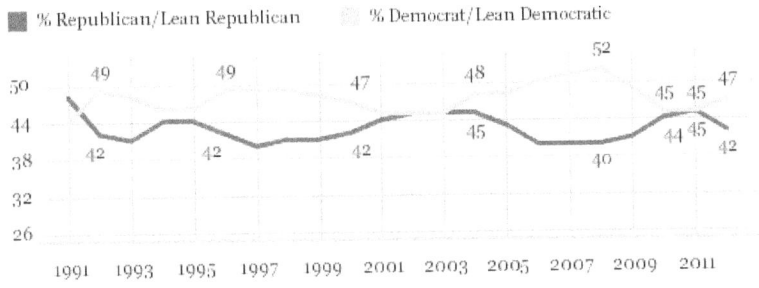

Figure 1.1: Gallup Poll of Party Leanings

A fundamental question that Christians must confront is whether we must be defined by one political ideology or the other. Must all Christians be conservative by the above definitions of conservatism? Is there a place for believers who hold to conservative moral values, and yet would not want to legislate righteousness for every citizen? During the 2012 vice-presidential debate, Joseph Biden said, concerning his stand on abortion, that his personal position stands with his Roman Catholic faith, which is a stance against abortion, yet he would not want to impose that belief on Muslims, Hindus, Buddhists, and other Americans who may not share his

---

24. Jones, "In U.S., Democrats Re-Establish Lead."

faith. This kind of position does not seem to go well with some within the evangelical Christian tradition. We seem to operate by the standard of "you are either in or you are out."

It must be established that political ideologies are not synonymous to Christian doctrines. Haidt defines ideology as "a set of beliefs about the proper order of society and how it can be achieved."[25] He quotes Karl Marx, who said that people choose ideologies to further their self-interest. If that is the case, it must be clear that political ideologies are not necessarily aligned with religious ideologies or doctrines. While political ideologies seek to promote certain self-interests, religious doctrines seek to pursue divine ends: heaven for Christians, Nirvana for Hindus, and self-realization for New Age people, for example. In view of these divergent goals, it behooves Christians to be careful to separate political ideologies from the Christian faith. We must be objective enough to look into the opposing political ideologies to identify principles that align with our faith, adopt and affirm them, while rejecting those that conflict with our faith and beliefs. The fact of the matter is that both the liberal and the conservative wings of the American political landscape contain elements we can agree and disagree with. Individuals who have articulated the unholy alliance inherent in full identification with one of these divergent views have settled with the term moderates. These people call themselves moderate conservatives or moderate liberals. The term *moderate* is problematic on its own as it suggests that one is holding to a middle ground on all these issues. What about those who would hold an extreme conservative position on one issue such as the constitutional right to bear arms, yet believe in the right of women to make abortion and birth control decisions? Are they still moderates? Is it possible for the church to empower her members to take a stand on issues, rather than give blind and uncritical allegiance to political ideologies or parties?

> Political ideologies are not synonymous to Christian doctrines.

When the evangelical church in America begins to remove herself from the current climate of unholy alliance with the Republican Party and establish her apolitical identity, she will position herself at a place where she can speak truth to both the Republican and the Democratic parties. No true Christian—who has Christ as Lord and Savior—can be one hundred percent conservative on all issues or one hundred percent liberal on

---

25. Haidt, "Born This Way?" 26.

all issues. When we begin to see the world through Christ's lenses and not through political lenses, multiculturalism will no longer appear to us as one bad liberal progressive agenda that is opposed to God and his church. To this end we undertake introducing multiculturalism to you, with the hope that you can suspend your political biases and engage it on its own merit, not as a liberal or conservative ideology, but as an idea, a process, and a reform movement.[26]

CHAPTER SUMMARY

In this chapter we have examined the impact political ideologies have had on the Christian responses to multiculturalism. Using these as background, we will move on to discuss the origin, development, and significance of multiculturalism as an ideology, and to present multicultural education as an idea and a movement. The subsequent chapters will discuss the goals of multicultural education and their significance for educational equity. We will then go to the Scriptures to investigate biblical foundations for multiculturalism, equity pedagogy, and praxis. Using biblical insights we will discuss shalom as (1) a new paradigm for multiculturalism, (2) as a kingdom motif for the educational setting, and (3) a kingdom motif for the twenty-first-century church.

---

26. Banks and McGee Banks, *Multicultural Education*.

2

Contemporary Thought on the Christian Worldview and the Implications for Multiculturalism

Multiculturalism has become a highly controversial topic that has emerged as a source of contention and conflicting opinions within the Christian community in the last couple of decades. As we are entering into the postmodern era, understanding and teaching diversity and multicultural issues have anchored more upon the activities of educators and teachers, with the church taking an almost passive stance on addressing the issues of multiculturalism. The goal of this chapter is to engage the views of some contemporary Christian minds on multiculturalism. This engagement is done with a mindset of presenting and critiquing these perspectives and using them as foundational materials for discussing what should be the nature of the Christian response to multiculturalism.

Among the select few whose thoughts on the Christian worldview we are engaging are R. C. Sproul, Charles Colson and Nancy Pearcey, Charles Kraft, Albert Wolters, Reinhold Niebuhr, Jon Newton, and Joseph Aldrich. These individuals have been selected exclusively on the basis of their written works. They may not necessarily represent the leading Christian voices on social and other related issues, but their works have significant content that we have deemed appropriate to reference in this book.

R. C. SPROUL, (1986). *LIFEVIEWS: MAKE A CHRISTIAN IMPACT ON CULTURE AND SOCIETY*

Born in Pittsburg, Pennsylvania, in 1939, Sproul is president of the Ligonier Academy of Biblical and Theological Studies and the founder and president of a ministry that began in 1971 as the Ligonier Valley Study Center in Ligonier, Pennsylvania. Ligonier Ministries today is an international multimedia ministry located near Orlando, Florida. Sproul has a daily radio broadcast called *Renewing Your Mind with Dr. R. C. Sproul.*

Sproul has written more than seventy books, not counting his many articles and lectures. One of his books that has been widely read is titled *Lifeviews*. In this book, Sproul sees the secularization of America as a postmodern phenomenon, which he also calls post-Christian. He engages the idea that, unlike many other cultures, America is not a uniform culture, but rather a cultural melting pot. Whereas he sees the melting pot ideology as positive, he warns of the apparent dangers that come with it. According to him, things get mixed up in a melting pot, and so when conflicting ideas are mixed up they become confusing ideas. He speaks of dominant cultural systems at work in America alongside subcultures.

A multicultural ideology that Sproul deals with in this book is pluralism. America's religious pluralistic environment has been the positive bedrock for the multicultural agenda in the educational and political arenas. Sproul, however, sees pluralism as antithetical to Christianity. Pluralism values and affirms divergent views, but Christianity is exclusionary in its religious values. According to Sproul, "Once a church embraces pluralism, it doesn't matter whether we agree on the essential points of the Christian faith, because it's all relative."[1] Let it be clear, however, that in this context Sproul sees pluralism as problematic when embraced as a way of looking at spirituality and the doctrines of the church, and hopefully not necessarily problematic as a socio-political ideology for a secular society. The challenge that arises from this perspective, however, is that multiculturalism not only advocates tolerance, it goes further to advocate appreciation of differences. The church should find it problematic to appreciate and affirm a religious doctrine or ideology that contradicts the Christian faith, but not a secular ideology that advocates tolerance and appreciation of cultural and individual differences.

---

1. Sproul, *Lifeviews.*

CHARLES COLSON AND NANCY PEARCEY, (1999). *HOW NOW SHALL WE LIVE?*

Charles Colson is described on Wikipedia as "a Christian leader, cultural commentator, and author of at least twenty books."[2] He was a former Special Counsel to President Richard Nixon and was implicated and incarcerated as part of the Watergate scandal, having pled guilty to obstruction of justice. He converted to Christianity shortly before going to prison and, upon leaving prison, spent his life working on prison ministry and serving as a public speaker. He died in 2012. One of his twenty books is titled *How Now Shall We Live?* This book is described as a radical challenge to the church and Christians to go beyond salvation and understand biblical faith as an entire worldview and perspective on life. Among other things, the book's goal was to expose false views and values of the modern culture. Modern culture, therefore, is a central focus of this book.

Nancy Pearcey was a policy director of the Wilberforce Forums, executive director of Charles Colson's daily radio program *BreakPoint*, and a coauthor of Colson's monthly column in *Christianity Today*. She is a fellow at the Discovery Institute's Center for the Renewal for Science and Culture, and managing editor of the journal *Origins and Designs*.

Colson and Pearcey argued that though we live in a pluralistic society, we serve a God who is sovereign over all. They argued that part of the Christian mandate is to reform or rebuild culture, to change laws, to conform to biblical standards of righteousness. Colson and Pearcey saw multiculturalism as a new form of Marxism. According to them, whereas in classic Marxism the oppressed were the proletariat, in multiculturalism the newer Marxism presents the oppressed as women, blacks, or homosexuals.[3] This tendency of painting multiculturalism as a newer form of Marxism is one of the most negative critiques of multiculturalism from a Christian leader. According to them, Marxism has been reborn "as multiculturalism and political correctness . . . [and] remains one of the most widespread and influential forms of counterfeit salvation."[4]

> *Colson and Pearcey saw multiculturalism as a new form of Marxism.*

---

2. "Charles Colson."
3. Colson and Pearcey, *How Now Shall We Live?* 233.
4. Ibid.

Colson and Pearcey's perspectives make multiculturalism anti-Christian, just as Marxism is. Unfortunately, that may not be an accurate and fair representation of multiculturalism. Yes, multiculturalism advocates political correctness, but political correctness does not mean endorsing what you oppose, but instead embracing a willingness to respect differences, a willingness to agree to disagree, and a willingness to accept the rights of others to be who they are even when that conflicts with your values and faith. There are biblical foundations for freedom of choice, worldview, and religious differences. In Joshua 24:14–15, the children of Israel were given a choice to worship God or go back to the idols that their forefathers worshipped before the call of Abraham. It was a choice then; it is a choice today; and it will always be a choice to serve God. In the New Testament, the apostle Paul demonstrated a willingness to respect and accept cultural differences even while fulfilling his mission of spreading the gospel of Jesus Christ (1 Cor 9:19–23).

ALBERT M. WOLTERS, (1985). *CREATION REGAINED: BIBLICAL BASIS FOR A REFORMATIONAL WORLDVIEW*

Albert Wolters is a professor of religion, theology, and classical studies at Redeemer University College in Ancaster, Ontario, Canada. Born in the Netherlands, his family immigrated to Canada when he was young. He is generally known for his *Creation Regained*, a book focusing on establishing and developing a "Reformational" Christian worldview. His other works include the following: *Plotinus: "On Eros": A Detailed Exegetical Study of Enneads III, 5; The Copper Scroll: Overview; Text and Translation; The Song of the Valiant Woman: Studies in the Interpretation of Proverbs 31:10–31*. He has also written a number of scholarly articles.

Wolters' thoughts as they apply to the topic of this book derive from his discussion of the Christian worldview in his *Creation Regained: Biblical Basis for a Reformational Worldview*. First he attempted to define *worldview*. Tracing it back to the German *Weltanschauung*, he identifies worldview as synonymous with "life-perspective" or "confessional vision." He defined *worldview* as "the comprehensive framework of one's basic beliefs about things."[5] He sees worldview as a matter of belief and argues that the basic beliefs one holds about things tend to form a framework or pattern, which consequently influence the way we act or behave. This argument is

---

5. Wolters, *Creation Regained*, 2.

significant as we engage the topic of multiculturalism because our beliefs and convictions about people who are different from us and about their ways of life have significant impact on how much we extend the love of God to them. Wolters identified two ways God imposes his law on the cosmos: directly without mediation, or indirectly through the involvement of human responsibility. Corresponding to these two laws are two ways of ruling, which he identifies as the laws of nature and norms.

Two Kinds of God's Ruling: Laws of Nature and Norms

There are two ways God imposes his law for His will to be done on earth: laws of nature and norms. Laws of nature include the laws of gravity, motion, thermodynamics, photosynthesis, chemistry, heredity—all the natural laws. God put the planets in their orbits, makes the seasons come and go at the proper time, makes seeds grow and animals reproduce. However, God entrusts to mankind the tasks of making tools, doing justice, producing arts, and pursuing scholarship. This is God's law for culture and society, which we call norms.[6] Therefore, God's rule of law is immediate in the non-human realm but God's norms are mediated by culture and society.

It is important to point out here that when using Wolters's thoughts as a foundational building block we can rightly argue that cultures and cultural diversity with their accompanying patterns and frameworks are God's creation. The laws of nature govern the earth as developed by God directly, in the so-called *creation secunda*; the norms govern the earth as developed by God indirectly, through people, in what we might call the *creation tertia*. Just as the eight creational "let there be's" represent creational law for the animal, vegetable, and mineral realms, so the fourfold "cultural mandate" represents creational law for society and culture.[7]

God appointed human beings to execute his commandments through cultural and social interventions. As co-laborers with God who are creatures made in his image, human beings have a measure of custody over the earth. There is nothing in human life that does not belong to the created order. Everything we are and do is thoroughly creature-like. First Timothy 4:3–4 states that everything God created is good and nothing is to be rejected. Romans 13:1–2 and 1 Peter 2:13–14 state that the existing authorities have been established by God, and Romans 13:1–5 states that civil authority

6. Ibid., 15.
7. Ibid., 36.

belongs to the created order; the state is founded as an ordinance of God. These incidental biblical givens merely illustrate a point that follows from the basic confession of the universal scope of God's ordinances.

Reformation of Culture through Sanctification

The effects of sin touch all of creation; no created thing is in principle untouched by the corrosive effects of the Fall. Everywhere we turn, the good possibilities of God's creation are misused, warped, and exploited for sinful ends. Distortion is perhaps most obvious in our individual lives, where the effects of the Fall are most readily recognized by Christians. The good handiwork of God in nature has been drawn into the sphere of human sinful mutiny against God (Rom 8:22).[8] Our cultural life provides many examples of the perversion of God's good creation. That the Fall is at the root of all evils is most clear for specifically human evil as it is manifested, for example, in personal, cultural, and societal distortions.[9] This renders even our cultures and worldviews in need of sanctification.

Two Stages of Redemption

Salvation is re-creation, not to imply that God scraps his earlier creation and in Jesus Christ makes a new one, but rather to suggest that he hangs on to his fallen original creation and salvages it. Humankind, which has botched its original mandate and the whole of creation along with it, is given another chance in Christ; we are reinstated as God's stewards on earth. How are we restored to the original (good) creation? Wolters identifies two stages of restoration: (1) sanctification and (2) progressive renewal.

The restoration of creation can only be accomplished through the death and resurrection of Jesus Christ. Sanctification is the process whereby the Holy Spirit, in and through the people of God, purifies creation from sin on the basis of Christ's atonement and victory. That purifying activity, that making holy, is a process that brings an inner renewal and revitalization of God's creatures and not just an external connection to the institutional church and its services of worship.[10]

8. Ibid., 44.
9. Ibid., 46.
10. Ibid., 74.

A second feature is that the avenue of this sanctification is a progressive renewal rather than a violent overthrow. This principle is particularly relevant at a societal and cultural plane, for it offers biblical strategy for social change or transformation (1 Thess 5:21). Social structures must be established to enhance the creative mandate of God. They must demonstrate the creative norm from inception. So Christians must oppose any distortions of God's handiwork. But such opposition must always affirm the proper and right exercise of responsibility in relation to other humans and the environment.

REINHOLD NIEBUHR (1951). *CHRIST AND CULTURE*

Niebuhr (1892–1971), sometimes described as the best-known Christian intellectual in the United States, began a career-long association with New York's Union Theological Seminary in 1928. He served as professor of Christian ethics (1928–1960) and dean (1950–1960). His most famous work is *Christ and Culture*. It is often referenced in discussions and writings on Christians' response to the world's culture. In this book, Niebuhr gives a history of how Christianity has responded to culture. He outlines five prevalent viewpoints:

- Christ against culture: Christ is the sole authority, and the claims of culture are to be rejected.

- Christ of culture: The Christian system is not different from culture in kind but only in quality; the best of culture should be selected to conform to Christ.

- Christ above culture: The reception of grace perfects and completes culture, though there is not a "smooth curve or continuous line" between them.

- Christ and culture in paradox: Both are authorities to be obeyed, and the believer, therefore, lives with this tension.

- Christ as transformer of culture: Culture reflects the fallen state of humanity; in Christ, humanity is redeemed and culture can be renewed so as to glorify God and promote his purposes.[11]

---

11. Niebuhr, *Christ and Culture*.

The main problem with Niebuhr is that he puts biblical authors and writings at odds with one another.[12]

Niebuhr's theory was updated by McGavran as he urged missionaries to take a high view of the Bible along with a high view of culture. McGavran categorized the relationship between Christianity and culture with four possible options:

1. A high view of the Bible and a low view of culture
2. A high view of culture and a low view of the Bible
3. A low view of the Bible and a low view of culture
4. A high view of the Bible and a high view of culture[13]

"A high view of Bible" means the entire Bible is the word of God. It is authoritative and demands faith and obedience to all its declarations. "A high view of culture" means that each culture is reasonable given the specific circumstances in which it has developed.

Charles Kraft, who is discussed next, built upon Niebuhr's work as he articulated his own thoughts on culture.

CHARLES H. KRAFT (1998). *CHRISTIANITY IN CULTURE: A STUDY IN DYNAMIC BIBLICAL THEOLOGIZING IN CROSS-CULTURAL PERSPECTIVE*

Charles Kraft was a missionary to Nigeria in the 1960s under the Brethren Church of the United States. His missionary career was rather short-lived and he entered the world of academics, emerging as one of the leading Christian voices in the field of cultural anthropology in the twentieth century. Kraft taught for many years at Fuller Theological Seminary in Pasadena, California, and is currently professor emeritus of anthropology and intercultural communication there. Kraft is the author of about twenty books on a variety of topics ranging from anthropology to spiritual warfare. His book *Christianity in Culture: A Study in Dynamic Biblical Theologizing in Cross-cultural Perspective* is the primary source of the ideas represented here.

---

12. Hesselgrave, *Communicating Christ Cross-Culturally.*
13. McGavran, *Christianity and Cultures;* cf. Kraft, *Christianity in Culture,* 50.

Multiculturalism

From Cultural Evolutionism to Cultural Validity

Charles Kraft may be the most positively disposed towards cultural validity and multiculturalism compared to all the Christian writers discussed in this chapter. Kraft suggests that we need to switch our perspective from cultural evolutionism to cultural validity. The cultural evolutionists, strongly influenced by the traditional ethnocentrism of Western culture, saw individual cultures mainly as illustrative of particular stages in a worldwide evolutionary sequence. They placed the more civilized culture at the top of their pyramid and evaluated cultures based on the values of white versus black, good versus evil, and superior versus inferior.[14] Kraft argues that we should be careful to evaluate a culture first in terms of its own values, goals, and foci before venturing to compare it (either positively or negatively) with any other culture. Instead of underscoring differences from absolute norms, the relativistic point of view recognizes the validity of every set of norms for the people whose lives are guided by them, and the values these represent.[15]

An essential difference between Kraft and the previous authors we have cited is the fact that he is a Christian cultural anthropologist, who has lived and worked among other cultural groups outside of Western societies, and has come to appreciate cultural differences, seeing them as positive not negative. Without using the word *multiculturalism*, Kraft articulates a strong Christian perspective of multiculturalism. According to Kraft, the concept of cultural validity is well explained in Bible where God is continually at work in every culture at all times (Acts 14:17). All cultures are essentially equal with respect to at least three things: (1) their adequacy for those immersed in them; (2) the pervasiveness of the expression of human sinfulness manifested in and through them; and (3) their potential usefulness as vehicles of God's interaction with humanity.[16]

Kraft recommends that, rather than moralizing about the good or bad in the given culture, we should accept the validity of that culture, whether or not our own set of values predisposes us to approve of the behavior of that culture (or individuals in it). The reason for the differences between cultures does not seem to lie in differences between people's fundamental reasoning processes but in the different premises on which such reasoning

---

14. Kraft, *Christianity in Culture*, 49
15. Ibid., 52.
16. Ibid.

rests and the basic categories that influence the judgment of different peoples.[17]

Now, it must be noted that Kraft was writing for Christian workers and missionaries who were leaving Western societies to enter non-Western cultural settings to serve God. The challenge comes when these variety of cultures now merge at America's own crossroads. Should the same response that Kraft advocates—in a cross-cultural missionary setting—not be applicable to the American multicultural context? For many years Christian workers have had a double standard in our response to cultural diversity: We see value in non-Western cultures when we leave our American comfort zones to enter their world, but when they leave their own comfort zone to enter ours, we tend to discard the respect and appreciation for their cultures that Kraft has advocated and instead we endorse a blind melting pot ideology that may not be viable in the twenty-first century. Kraft presents a more *theocentric* view of culture, which should inform our response to multiculturalism. He articulates the idea of *human beings as God's partners,* and the idea of *the process of cultural transformation.*

Redeemed Human Beings as God's Partner

What is the relationship between God and culture? Kraft positions God as above culture—he is absolute, infinite, and exists totally outside of human culture—but God uses culture as the vehicle for interaction with human beings.[18] In other words, God assigned his power and authority to human beings, the redeemed ones, who are empowered to sustain the world as he commanded through a cultural mandate. Therefore, culture is a mediator (or what Kraft calls a communication channel), between the One, who is outside of culture, and humans, who are inside it. Even though God exists outside of culture, he intervenes in human history indirectly through the allegiances of redeemed human beings whose goals are to live for the sake of their master, Jesus Christ.[19]

---

17. Ibid., 113.
18. Ibid., 114.
19. Ibid., 345.

Multiculturalism

The Process of Cultural Transformation

When the redeemed in partnership with God engage in the process of cultural transformation, there is a transcendent goal that differs from that of a transformational change motivated by some other set of values. The goal is to enhance and increase the suitability of the given culture as a vehicle for divine-to-human interaction.[20] The goal should be true transformational change, as opposed to mere superficial external alteration.[21] This is first a matter of change in the central conceptualizations (worldview) of a culture. The centrality of worldview to culture and its functions, with its concomitant conservatism, raises one set of problems with regard to any attempt to transform it. It is this worldview that undergirds a culture/subculture's perceived reality. It also governs its people's output or response to that reality. When change occurs in that worldview, its effects send ripples throughout the rest of the cultural structures.[22]

With respect to attempts to bring about change at the worldview level, a basic problem of the transformational approach is how to keep the pressure on change while at the same time assuring that such change will be minimally traumatic. A second fact raises even bigger problems: any disequilibrium at the center of a culture radiates strongly through the cultural structures. If some major aspect of a people's worldview comes under attack from without, or suspicion arises from within the culture, the effects of such disequilibrium will manifest themselves in many areas of the people's thoughts and behaviors.

Given the power of worldview and cultural structures in shaping people's lives and coping mechanisms, we must sound a clarion call for professing Christians to tread cautiously when encountering people from other cultures. The demand that they drop their cultural heritage and melt into our Anglo-Saxon Western culture is not only unrealistic but also offensive, and it denies their sense of personhood and self-determination. Multiculturalism must be seen as an attempt to affirm those who are different from us, stepping outside of our comfort zones to get to know them for who they really are.

---

20. Ibid., 351.
21. Ibid., 347.
22. Haught, "Former Multnomah U. President 'Dr. Joe' Aldrich Dies."

JOSEPH ALDRICH (1981). *LIFE-STYLE EVANGELISM*

Joseph Aldrich (1941–2009) was president of the neo-evangelical Multnomah School of the Bible in Portland, Oregon, which became Multnomah University. He was known for his book *Life-Style Evangelism*, and its ideas of culture provide the basis for his inclusion in this section. Among his other books are *Secrets to Inner Beauty*, *Self-Worth*, and *Love for All Your Worth*. Aldrich is described online as "highly ecumenical in his approach to evangelism."[23] He freely cites a variety of Christian authors among which are C. S. Lovett, Peter Wagner, Charles Swindoll, Billy Graham, Luis Palau, and Bill Bright.

His thoughts on culture as expressed in *Lifestyle Evangelism* anchor on the idea that throughout the history of Christianity the church has responded to the relationship between conversion and human culture in at least four ways: rejection, immersion, split adaptation, and critical participation.

Rejection

This is a lifestyle of withdrawal and isolation, not limited to monastic orders or religious sects. It is not uncommon among Christians in many of our churches. Aldrich sees this as a "closed corporation" mentality, a sort of Christian isolationism, which has been a constant barrier to evangelism. Many Christians have been so afraid of being contaminated by worldliness that they have avoided any social contacts with unconverted persons. As a result, they have no natural bridge for evangelism; what witnessing they do is usually artificial and forced rather than the spontaneous outgrowth of genuine friendship.

Such rejectionists develop their own language, values, customs, and social activities. Social segregation from the non-Christian world is normative for them. A radical difference must be maintained. The unbeliever is to be avoided at all costs. This may appear an overstatement, perhaps, but not without basis. Because of their emphasis upon only a radical difference, they have a message, but no audience.

Sadly, many evangelical churches, while not espousing monastic isolationism, have become isolationist nonetheless, limiting their engagement to those who look like them, act like them, and see the world as they do.

---

23. Aldrich, *Life-Style Evangelism*.

Multiculturalism

Immersion

Aldrich sees this as the exact opposite of rejection. Some Christians, sensing the need for a radical identification with human culture (the world) fail to maintain the radical difference so important to the rejectionist. As a result, they become essentially indistinguishable from the world. Reflective of this kind of faith is the Unitarian Universalist Church, which discards all creed and dogma, and individual perspectives rule. Their salt loses its saltiness and effective evangelism ceases. They have an audience, but no unified message. These believers succumb to the world's pressures, allowing it to push them into its mold. They become like the world and lose their message for the world. This must be the context where Sproul's argument that pluralism is anti-Christian must be given serious consideration.

Split Adaptation

According to Aldrich, a third response of Christianity to culture is split adaptation. This view is a blend of the rejection and immersion options. In reality it is a form of spiritual schizophrenia. This person is a citizen of two worlds and attempts to be at home in both of them. Like the rejectionist, he strongly criticizes human cultures as being tainted by sin, transient, and without redeeming value. Yet he adapts by conforming to the very world he denies. He drifts with the majority opinion and experiences varying degrees of discomfort. The thought of bringing his faith to bear on the social ills and injustices of his culture never crosses his mind. He has so compromised the "radical difference" that it is neither radical nor different any longer. Association with the non-Christian community is usually viewed as necessary compromise. He is in it (of necessity) but not of it, having accepted Christ as Lord.

Critical Participation

A dual citizen of heaven and earth, this believer knows that God has him involved in a redemptive mission with cultural implications. He does not believe that new birth should "de-culturalize" a new believer. Believers are to be spiritually distinct from the world's culture, but not socially segregated from it. The believer is in the world, but not of the world. A conflict arises as the redeemed and unredeemed cultures collide in their attempts to lay claims on the life of the new believer.

Paul faced the problem of conflicting cultural standards in Rome and Corinth. Some in the Christian community refused to buy or eat meat offered to pagan idols, while others felt free to buy and eat such meat. Conflict was inevitable. Paul's answer to the problem was to the point. Both views were right, depending on the individual's conscience before the Lord. For one, eating was sin, for another, it was not sin. But the non-meat eater had to remember that there was nothing inherently wrong with the meat because it had been offered to nonexistent deities. The conscience-stricken, non-meat eater's response was correct in that he should not violate his conscience. And the meat eater had to be cautious, not because his actions were wrong, but because of the possibility of creating confusion on the part of the weaker brother (cf. Rom 14:1–4, 13–23; 1 Cor 8:1–13).

The critical participators live with the perpetual tension between Christian faith and human culture. Although they are not deceived by promises of utopia on earth, they know that they can be God's instruments to work in and through cultural institutions to bring people to Christ. They view their life mission as obeying God and demonstrating loving concern for people and the structures and institutions in which they live and function.

According to Aldrich, a balance between a critical transcendence (radical difference) and a concerned cultural participation (radical identification) must be maintained. The key seems to be maintaining a balance between the believer's radical difference and his radical identification. Our radical difference is holiness (wholeness)—not legalism or externalism. Only holiness makes radical identification a legitimate option for the Christian. At conversion, the new Christian usually moves from cultural immersion towards radical difference. To become effective in evangelism one must move back towards the old culture, not to re-immerse oneself, but to become radically (and receptively) identified with it (unsaved people). Although our Lord expects communication without contamination, we cannot communicate effectively without contact (identification).

Multiculturalism

JON NEWTON (2004). "THE CHALLENGE OF POSTMODERNITY"

Jon Newton's article "The Challenge of Postmodernity" was published in J. Ireland's *Pointing the Way: Directions for Christian Education in a New Millennium*. Some of Newton's basic assertions, which are critical for our consideration, include the fact that in the postmodern era, Christians cannot present the gospel in quite the same way as in the 1950s and 1960s. We face a practical challenge to present the eternal gospel of Christ as the Way, Truth, and the Life, when postmodernism is suspicious of any claims to truth as absolute, timeless, or built on culture-free foundations. It sees all truth claims as "perspectival," that is, influenced and biased by the cultural, political, and personal perspective of the person making the claim. Newton states that propositions that seemed self-evident to a Western mind in one culture and context may make little sense in other cultures and contexts. Culture as seen from the postmodern view has meant, among many things, a "breakdown of the differences between 'highbrow' and popular expressions of culture" and "a revival of 'old-fashioned' styles in opposition to the modern."[24] Newton states that postmodernist thinking has infected all walks of life, including religion and all fields of education. The effects on education are seen in the following areas:

1. Redefinition of educational terms or a questioning of their usefulness, often on a political basis.

2. Rewriting of history to restore the suppressed history of minorities such as women or the LGBT community.

3. Teachers openly promoting their political, moral, or social views to students. Since it is impossible to be unprejudiced or objective, according to postmodernism, teachers should promote views openly and honestly but not be intolerant.

4. Promotion of values such as tolerance, intuition, diversity, and multiculturalism above reason or moral absolutes, for example, teaching of alternative lifestyles and acceptance of each person's sexual preference.

5. Promotion of a constructivist view of truth or knowledge by which no answers are wrong; everything is relative to society, and pragmatic

---

24. Newton, "The Challenge of Postmodernity," 184.

and group-oriented standards take the place of rational criteria for decision-making.[25]

A critical view of Newton's analysis from a Christian perspective will indeed justify a tepid response to postmodernism's ideas and principles from the church. This is more so in light of its promotion of moral relativism. It is understandable that any sincere Christian would have issues with the promotion of any non-Christian value "above reason or moral absolutes," especially when such values conflict with our deeply held doctrines and beliefs. The question is whether multiculturalism, which Newton has linked to postmodernism, is indeed advocating that cultural and social values be seen as above reason and moral absolutes.

CHAPTER SUMMARY

Multiculturalism has been defined as an "idea, a process, and a reform movement"[26] that advocates that diversity of people groups, cultural groups, and worldviews are seen as positive and legitimate social realities, rather than seen as outside the norm. Diversity needs to be seen as credible and valid even within Christian circles. Multiculturalism acknowledges people's rights to be different and still remain credible. It advocates their rights to see things differently from the way others see them, including choosing to believe in non-absolutes. Does that pose a major challenge to the Christian worldview? Certainly it does. Yet the challenge is one the gospel is capable of engaging and overcoming. The Christian gospel did not shy away from the Greco-Roman culture of the first century AD; instead it transformed it.

Certain aspects of multicultural ideas and ideals must be given an objective Christian critique. On what grounds can any well-meaning child of God question the need for (1) the restoration of the suppressed history of minorities in America and (2) the promotion of values such as justice, tolerance, diversity, and multiculturalism?

A sad truth that the Christian community must be willing to confront is that America's track record on the rights of minorities—whether Native Americans, African Americans, the Chinese, Japanese, other ethnicities, or women—has been less than commendable. Every one of these people groups was represented in the garden of Eden when God said, "Let us make

---

25. Newton, "The Challenge of Postmodernity."
26. Banks and McGee Banks, *Multicultural Education*, 3.

Multiculturalism

man in our image, in our likeness, and let them rule over the fish of the sea and the birds of the air, over all the creatures that move along the ground" (Gen 1:26). God made "them" one race of human beings, plural in gender, yet one in race. Part of our fallen state has led to the ethnic and gender separations that have brought about so much unrest within the race of humans. Part of the redeeming message is a restoration of humankind to the original state of oneness with God and with one another. So an ideology that advocates a restoration of the rights of ethnic and gender minorities cannot be outside of the Christian frame of reference.

Even as this argument is stretched to include liberal perspectives on sexual orientation and related topics, it must be clearly stated that freewill is a gift of God, and nowhere in the Bible are Christians called to legislate righteousness. We have our rights to object to certain lifestyles based on our interpretation of the Bible, but we have no rights to legislate righteousness for anyone. Multiculturalism requires us to be willing to respect people's choices and decisions, even when we do not agree with them. Those who have issues with our rights to disagree with certain lifestyles certainly abound, and they may be vocal about it. Nevertheless, that does not make them the spokespeople for multiculturalism at the expense of others who may not share their extreme views but still hold to the rights of all people to live their lives as they please.

Joshua and the people of Israel exemplified this right to divergent choices and worldviews when, in Joshua 24:1–15, Joshua called upon the people of Israel, a people to whom God had revealed himself in all kinds of miracles and to whom he had given a land of promise, wherein they now settled in peace. Joshua told them that despite all they knew about God and all the benefits they had received from God, they had a choice to decide to worship and serve him or go after the gods of the Canaanites. Belief in and worship of God has always been a free will decision. It should never be mandated nor imposed on humans. This is a God-given right and liberty.

Diversity is a creation of God. Gender diversity began in the Garden of Eden as part of God's plan for humanity (Gen 1:27–28; 2:18–25). Ethnic diversity, though often attributed to sin and the fallen nature, in its essence reflects the creative marvels of God. The entire human race is redeemable, and all cultures are redeemable. Within the family of God, diversity becomes an asset rather than a liability. So a critical look at the ideas presented in this chapter reveals the fact that an uncritical dismissal of multiculturalism as a postmodern ideology is not only erroneous but also dangerous as it quickly closes the door to a Christian attempt to define multiculturalism in a way that is redeeming and God-honoring.

3

The Facts and Fallacies of the Christian Views on Multiculturalism

As long as multiculturalism has been studied, multiple voices expressing different views have ranged from educators to social and political activists to researchers. This chapter focuses on the facts and fallacies of the Christian views of multiculturalism as Marxist ideology, postmodern ideology, critical pedagogy, and liberation theology.

MULTICULTURALISM AS A MARXIST IDEOLOGY

In Marxist theory, human society consists of two parts: the base and the superstructure. The former consists of the forces of production, while the latter strengthens the base such as culture, institutions, political power structures, roles and rituals. Culture is a signifying system deeply embedded in its material base.[1] Those two parts are united closely in a state in order to control and govern the people. Although the base determines the course of human history, Marx proclaimed the importance of the role of the superstructure whose role is to create appropriate ideologies in order to perpetuate the dominant social order. That's why Marxists pay close attention to the role of schooling through which ideologies are shaped and propagated.[2] For example, Althusser, an Italian neo-Marxist, distin-

---

1. McLaren and Farahmandpur, *Teaching against Global Capitalism*.
2. Gi, "Postmodernism and Marxism."

guishes between the Ideological State Apparatus (ISA) and the Repressive State Apparatus (RSA).[3] The latter functions by violent and repressive power whereas the former functions by ideological and symbolic power. The school system is seen as the most strategic and effective of ISAs in propagating the ideology of the dominant group. The state is also seen as employing its sovereign powers to seek increasing bureaucratic control of teaching and curricula.[4]

The questions we must confront within the limits of this discourse are as follows: Is multiculturalism derived from the Marxist ideology? Are there any similarities between the two? The answer to these questions, to some extent, may be yes. Some proponents of multiculturalism tend to see the world as a dichotomy, and they focus on the power struggle between the social majority and social minority, the "haves" and the "have-nots," the oppressors and the oppressed in a given society. In the U.S. educational setting, the main focus is on ethnic minority students or other disadvantaged student populations that are neglected or marginalized in the school systems. In this perspective, the history of multiculturalism is the story of the victims who have been discriminated against, who are eventually gaining access to resources and power in society.[5]

Marxism argues that the working class (proletariat) has been mistreated through formal education and schooling. It asks the working class to transform society. The goal of Marxist theory is not only to explain the world but also to transform it. In the same way, multiculturalism is seen as an educational movement for social transformation. James and Cheryl McGee Banks included in their definition of multicultural education the idea that multicultural education is a "reform movement that is trying to change the schools and other educational institutions so that students from all social-class, gender, racial, language, and cultural groups will have an equal opportunity to learn."[6] Multicultural educators, therefore, have a set of expectations in which schools are supposed to be structured to enable all students to learn and succeed regardless of the differences of gender, cultures, and ethnicities. Marxism posits the human being as an active being, one who can change his world.[7] The transformational

3. Althusser, *Lenin and Philosophy and Other Essays.*
4. Gi, "Postmodernism and Marxism."
5. D'Souza, *Illiberal Education.*
6. Banks and McGee Banks, *Multicultural Education,* 4.
7. Brown, *Toward a Maerxist Psychology.*

Multiculturalism

ideology underlying multiculturalism can rightfully be said to be similar to Marxism in philosophy, but not necessarily to share the same goals and avenues for transformation. Furthermore, both Marxism and multiculturalism share the vision of a future society in which everyone enjoys equal and fair opportunities and are governed by even and fair rules. The difference is that while Marxism advocates a classless society, multiculturalism does not. Rather, it advocates equal access for all. Educational interventions towards fulfilling the vision of equal access and equal opportunities are considered critical in multicultural education.

It is important to note that part of the original purpose of the educational system was to prepare future generations for adaptation within a continually changing occupational environment, a goal that is not too difficult to visualize in a highly industrialized setting.[8] Beyond occupational adaptation, it is important to note that the purpose of education is for the common good. The power and prospect of education to change individual lives and societies cannot be overemphasized.[9] This idea of common good underlies Marxist ideology. So to this degree, there is certainly an overlap between these views.

There are some clear differences, however, between Marxism and multiculturalism. Whereas multiculturalism desires to work through the existing social structures, transforming and enhancing them to make them more effective in meeting the needs of all, Marxism desires to dismantle the old and replace it with the new. Whereas multiculturalism desires to empower the weak so they can become as strong as those who already possess power, Marxism desires to weaken the strong so as to empower the weak. Multiculturalism, therefore, desires mutual benefits, while Marxism seeks to benefit the proletariat at the expense of the bourgeoisie. The idea of class struggle so prevalent in Marxist thinking is not so in multiculturalism. It focuses not so much on class struggles as on equal opportunities for social mobility and access. The goal of Marxist educators is to prevent the dominant class from taking over everything; multicultural education, however, advocates mutual empowerment towards success, not necessarily preventing anyone from growth.[10] The Marxist ideology of a classless society is not necessarily the

---

8. Leonhard, *Three Faces of Marxism*, 39.
9. DomNwachukwu, "Through the Eyes of Faith."
10. Gi, "Postmodernism and Marxism."

goal of multiculturalism; rather, it aims for equal access for all classes of society, so that people can rise to opportunities without socially imposed restrictions.

So yes, multiculturalism shares certain historical interests with Marxism, but remains significantly different from it in the nature of its goals and the means by which those goals are pursued.

MULTICULTURALISM AS POSTMODERNISM

In an article titled "Christianity, Science, and Postmodernism," Sean Devine attempted to define postmodernism, seeing it as a way of viewing the world that has resulted from disillusionment with an overoptimistic modern worldview that followed the intellectual developments of the Age of Enlightenment. Devine argued that the postmodern worldview is characterized by an assumption that many of today's power structures and values are grounded in the arrogant confidence of the Enlightenment that consolidates power rather than liberates. Postmodernism takes issue with the modernist scientific approach to explaining the universe, which is rather exclusionary rather than inclusive. Postmodernism is more inclusive than exclusive in defining source of knowledge. This inclusiveness informs the way all of reality, including social issues and challenges, is confronted.

Contemporary multiculturalism as a self-conscious movement in America is a byproduct of postmodernism, but multiculturalism as an intuitive, undefined practice and perspective has existed since ancient times. It was essential to the growth of early Christianity.

Social scientists have identified three waves of enlightenment: premodernism, modernism, and postmodernism. The major characteristics of each historical enlightenment paradigm are documented in the table 3.1:

Multiculturalism

Table 3.1: Historical Enlightenment Paradigm

Premodernism Greece/Rome to the Middle Ages	**Modernism** Middle Ages to the Twentieth Century	**Postmodernism** The Present
Dualism (secular and divine; idealism and rationalism). Faith and religion played central roles. Effective change; efforts were based on prayer, faith, thinking, and reasoning.	Empiricism, logical scientific methodology. Identification of objective truths and validity. Scientific and professional knowledge are displayed as the legitimate source of truth. Discovering truth comes via the logical process of science. Scientific knowledge is presented as the unique image of objective reality.	Creation of personal and social realities. The nature of meaning is relative. Phenomena are context-based. The process of knowledge and understanding is social, inductive, hermeneutical, and qualitative. New age, constructivism, multiculturalism are featured.

Postmodernism claims that there is no objective reality and denies absolute truth. Knight identified the characteristics of postmodernism: First, postmodernism rejects behaviorism with its scientific objectivity and technological approach to human engineering. Second, it also largely rejects the positivistic and objective views of philosophical analysis. However, postmodern theories respond positively to certain analytic philosophers due to their sensitivity to language and the interconnectedness of the meaning of the language.[11]

It is important, however, to recognize the fact that postmodernism is not anti-religious. It is more positively disposed towards religion than modernism. Whereas modernism—represented by modern science—sees rational knowledge expressed with scientific premises as absolute and exclusive, postmodernism embraces a plurality of sources of knowledge that does not exclude the sacred. Postmodernism has been defined as "a way of recognizing that the world is in a period of transition. It is a world 'that has not yet discovered how to define itself in terms of what *is*, but only in terms of what it has *just-now-ceased to be*.'"[12]

Socially, postmodernism spurs cultural movements that welcome plurality. To its credit, whereas modernity "brought with it the secular; post

---

11. Knight, *Philosophy and Education*, 92.

12. Adams, "Toward a Theological Understanding of Postmodernism," 520, quoting Toulmin, *Return to Cosmology*, 213.

modernity is restoring the sacred."[13] This is clearly evident in the cultural and religious revivals that have greeted the twenty-first century. These revivals span cultures, regions, and religious expressions. There is a strong affirmation of plurality, which has emerged as a hallmark of postmodernism. The challenge for Christianity rests in the prospects that postmodernism offers non-Christian religions. Strassberg sums it up: "postmodernity not only has room for religion but also provides conditions favorable for the development of 'new' forms of religious expressions."[14] Whereas the affirmation of plurality presents a threat to Christianity, an exclusive religion, it also presents opportunities that must not be overlooked. It presents a credible context for meaningful Christian evangelization in an environment where religion is seen as a valid and credible experience. Stuart Bate writes, "Salvation in Christ is good news for all and Christians are required to proclaim the *kerygma* wherever they can. This important evangelistic dimension of the Church is not negated by post-modern critique."[15] It was, however, significantly negated by the modernist scientific views.

Postmodernism deeply permeates the educational structures, as well as how we have come to understand and know reality and the nature of truth.[16] The postmodern era opens up new opportunities to rethink the processes of knowing and the nature of pedagogy in unique ways. Knight summarizes the influences of postmodernism on education with the following six points:

1. It is impossible to determine objective truth.
2. Language does not put us in contact with reality.
3. Language and meaning are socially constructed.
4. Metanarratives are social constructions developed by dominant groups to legitimate their position and privileges.
5. Knowledge is power.
6. Schools have traditionally functioned as agents of that power for social control via the manipulation of knowledge.[17]

---

13. Ibid.
14. Strassberg, "Magic, Religion, Science, Technology, and Ethics," 307–22.
15. Bate, "The Church and the Culture," 19–33.
16. Savery and Duffy, "Problem Based Learning"; Knight, *Philosophy and Education*.
17. Knight, *Philosophy and Education*, 95.

Multiculturalism

So in response to the question of whether multiculturalism is a byproduct of postmodernism, the resounding response is definitely yes. Multiculturalism originates from a postmodern perspective of inclusiveness. Postmodern thought is aligned with multiculturalism by promoting values such as tolerance, intuition, and diversity above strict moral and cultural absolutes.[18] Multicultural educators embrace cultural pluralism in which they assume that all cultures are valid, and there is no ideal or standard culture.

There are some differences in how Marxists and postmodernists view education. Gi breaks down these differences:

Table 3.2: Marxist and Postmodern Educators[19]

Marxist Educators	Postmodern Educators
• Assume that schools are continuing to reproduce unfair and unjust institutions • Insists that ideologies shape schooling • Anticipate more directive and political roles from educational researchers. • The educational researchers and teachers have to seek a kind of knowledge that will help students recognize the social function of particular forms of knowledge in order to provide students with a model that permits them to examine the underlying political, social, and economic foundations of the larger society and enable them to realize that the institutional power produces unequal and unjust educational policies. • Understand that people who have knowledge have power. • Question how dominant groups control the curriculum distribution and search how ideology shapes teachers and education	• Assume that schooling is contingently constructed and reconstructed by various technologies of power and knowledge • Assume that their role is not to tell or direct students as to what knowledge and truth are, or how to act and solve problems, but to analyze the present situation and to understand what has constructed school policies. • View knowledge as produced by power relations only. • Question why a specific group is included or excluded and look at how various knowledge productions constitute the notion of the teacher

It is important, therefore, that when Christian thinkers attempt to dismiss multiculturalism on the basis of its being a postmodern ideology, that we are careful to not readily dismiss multiculturalism on that basis. Postmodernism is not essentially anti-Christian, so aligning multiculturalism with it does not make it anti-Christian. Multicultural principles of equal opportunities and inclusiveness have sound biblical foundations and may not necessarily be opposed to Christian principles and values.

---

18. Newton, "The Challenge of Postmodernity."
19. Adapted from Gi, "Postmodernism and Marxism," 9–10.

MULTICULTURALISM AS CRITICAL PEDAGOGY

Critical pedagogy is an approach through which "students and teachers are encouraged to view what they learn in a critical light."[20] It has sparked an educational movement to encourage students and learners develop their consciousness for freedom and power in order to transform an unjust and unequal society. Even though critical pedagogy became popular with Paulo Freire's book *Pedagogy of the Oppressed* (1970), some researchers and educators have criticized critical pedagogy as being essentialist, populist, and unpatriotic.[21] The first criticism argues that critical pedagogy assumes that all students are oppressed. Secondly, there are some educators who argue that critical pedagogy is for the marginalized groups such as workers, those who are racially and culturally discriminated against, and/or women. Lastly, some "right-wing" educators accuse critical pedagogy of being unpatriotic because critical pedagogists empower students as catalysts of social dissent and change.

While there are differing approaches to and practices of critical pedagogy, some commonalities appear. First, most critical pedagogists have criticized the function of schooling as a social reproduction agent that perpetuates the existing social structure.[22] Second, the critical pedagogists claim that the eternal goal of education is "emancipation" from an oppressive and unequal society. In order to liberate from the reproductive function of a school, critical pedagogists offer a theoretical framework with a commensurate praxis designed to confront educational policies and mainstream discourses. Lastly, critical pedagogists claim that education cannot be divorced from politics.[23] Critical pedagogists always analyze the system of social oppression before setting up an educational intervention for social justice.

CRITICAL PEDAGOGY

Some people have seen multiculturalism as an intrinsic byproduct of critical pedagogy. This section will address three theories of critical pedagogy: pedagogy of praxis, reproduction theory, and radical multiculturalism.

20. Nieto, "School Reform and Student Learning," 401–20.
21. Chege, "Literacy and Hegemony."
22. Knight, *Philosophy and Education*.
23. Chege, "Literacy and Hegemony."

Multiculturalism

Critical pedagogy is grounded in the understanding of the origins and underpinnings of power in society, expressly angry at the flagrant abuse of power and injustices that are evident in various forms of human rights violations.[24] According to Steinberg, critical pedagogy is a transgressive discourse, practice, and fluid way of seeing the world in a continual attempt of the pedagogists to redefine both themselves (and the world) in the context they find themselves. Those engaged in critical pedagogy don't need to agree with one another, rather they need to engage in what she called a "radical fire of discursive disagreement."[25] According to Giroux, critical pedagogy has the task of educating students to become critical agents who actively "question and negotiate the relationships between theory and practice, critical analysis and common sense, learning and social change."[26] He argues that such pedagogy should cultivate in students a healthy skepticism about power so they are able to temper any reverence for authority with a sense of critical awareness.

Critical pedagogy and postmodernism share some common elements. First, like postmodernism, critical pedagogy is built on the premise that knowledge making is a complex process in which the social world is a conceptual landmine wired with assumptions and inherited meaning. Second, critical pedagogy's rejection of banking education (i.e., the view of education as a top-down transfer of knowledge from teacher to students) and the call for a dialogue approach concurs with postmodern recognition of knowledge as a social construct in which teachers and students collaborate in the knowledge-making process. Third, the paradigm advocates a pragmatic approach to praxis by underscoring the historicity of phenomenon.[27]

The two approaches have significant epistemological and ontological differences. Critical pedagogy adopts a humanistic approach informed by the belief that success of the liberation agenda depends on faith in the potential of students and teachers to discern social contradictions, along with faith in their desire to change their material conditions and create a just and equitable society. Postmodernism is inadequate for the task of rewriting the emancipating possibilities of the language and practice of a revitalized democratic public life. Therefore the main difference is the central role praxis plays. Unlike postmodernism, critical pedagogy anchors upon

---

24. Strassburg, "Magic, Religion, Science, Technology, and Ethics," ix.
25. Steinberg, "Where are We Now?" ix–x.
26. Giroux, "Democracy, Education," 1.
27. Chege, "Literacy and Hegemony."

the belief that theory must not go without praxis, and on the belief that students have the capacity to challenge the status quo if well equipped with what Freire calls "conscientization."

Pedagogy of Praxis

Pedagogy of praxis grounds its principles on the concept of liberation, coming from the Latin American liberation theology movement of the 1970s. Education is not a theory, but a strong weapon to accomplish the goal of liberation in Latin America. For Paulo Freire (1921–1977), liberation is the praxis of the people's action/reflection on their world in order to transform it. He viewed education as a process of liberation in community through *conscientization*, in which learners perceive the social, economic, and political contradictions around them and take action against oppressive elements.

The learning process had a dialogue-based, problem-posing format as Freire formulated that all-adult learners share, learn, and reflect upon their experiences based on their contextual realities.[28] Cannan identified three characteristics of dialogue-based, problem-posing pedagogy: First, dialogue is the center of the pedagogical process in which learners and teachers are co-investigators. This learning process, which stresses the learners' experience and expression, reversed the traditional top-down model of teaching (the banking model) in which one who knows (the teacher) imparts knowledge to one who is presumed ignorant.[29]

Second, it focuses on the situations in which the oppressed live and operate. The learning based on the learners' experiences and contexts brings them to a critical consciousness. In fact, pedagogy of praxis has its roots in the adult literacy program in Brazil in which Freire worked for many years. When Freire taught reading and writing to a Brazilian adult population, he assumed that the peasants he was working with were intelligent adults even though they lacked the linguistic tools of reading and writing. Education for them became a liberating tool that empowers them to live a more fulfilling life.

Lastly, in critical pedagogy teachers encourage students to change the world. Teachers take students' thoughts seriously and consider the students to be agents capable of expanding their understanding, empowering

---

28. Freire, *Pedagogy of the Oppressed*.
29. Cannan, "Developing a Pedagogy of Critical Hope," 159–74.

Multiculturalism

them to transform the unjust, repressive society. Throughout the process, the teacher enhances students' critical conscientiousness of the power dynamics that had prevented them from fully realizing their humanity. The learning output is gradually expanded to the process by which learners are educated into the fullness of the human condition.[30]

To what extent, therefore, has pedagogy of praxis impacted multiculturalism? Contextualized pedagogical practices have influenced multiculturalism. For example, when Freire taught the peasants, he redesigned all learning materials based on their lives and experiences. The learners (peasants) used words and images from the adult world of their own lives: their crops, tools, customs, referring even to issues of conflict and power like land tenure.[31] This very approach is easily transferable to other socio-cultural contexts. For generations American education has been Eurocentric. American history has been mostly history of the Americans of European descent. Pedagogy of praxis calls for an educational culture that is conscious of contextual factors affecting learning. The socio-cultural conditions of the learner, his/her own history and cultural experiences must become essential components of the learning experiences. Imperialistic education that presents learners with constructs, ideas and facts that are detached from their personal experiences are inadequate. Multiculturalism demands that education be contextualized in both its content and practices.

Reproduction Theory

The current educational setting has been severely criticized as inadequate. Researchers even argue that the current model of schooling has failed.[32] They argue that schooling in a capitalistic society exists for reproducing the current social system. Two approaches of reproduction theory are identified: social reproduction theory and cultural reproduction theory.

According to Bowles and Gintis, the school system helps the capitalistic society reproduce unequal, repressive, and exploitative social relations. Schooling is an instrument through which one reproduces the social order by socializing students to assume their appropriate places within a

---

30. Ferm, *Contemporary American Theologies*, 63.
31. Berryman, *Liberation Theology*.
32. E.g., Freire, *Politics of Education*; Giroux, *Teachers as Intellectuals*; Greene, *Dialectics of Freedom*; hooks, *Teaching to Transgress*; Kozol, *Shame of the Nation*.

capitalistic work order.³³ Reich explains that schooling was much like the mass production of the manufacturing system.³⁴ Students were like empty vessels to be filled with knowledge and skills. Without considering students' different backgrounds, learning styles, and prerequisite levels, all students were closely supervised, and uniformity, control, and centralization were core virtues in the schools. Under this paradigm, schools were merely institutions that prepared young people for their place in a competitive market economy by providing them basic skills such as reading, writing, and arithmetic—capabilities to meet the needs of the mass production assembly. The educational encounters invite students to accept the degree of powerlessness they will face as experienced workers.

Other educational theorists explain school's reproduction of the existing dominant structure from the cultural perspective (cultural reproduction theorists). For example, Bourdieu claims that variations in cultural capital reproduce educational inequality in schools.³⁵ In a classroom, the cultural capital of students who occupy subordinate class positions is systematically devalued. Bourdieu identifies three different forms of cultural capital that are acquired in the combined realms of upper-class families and strengthened through the school systems. Those three cultural capitals are embodied, objectified, and institutionalized: (1) an embodied type refers to both inherited and acquired properties of one's self; (2) the objectified cultural type exists in material objects and media including writings, paintings, monuments, instruments; (3) institutionalized capital is associated with an academic degree that consists of institutional recognition. The institutionalized cultural capital plays the most prominent role especially in the labor market because it allows a wide array of cultural capital to be expressed in a single qualitative and quantitative measurement.³⁶

Michael Apple emphasized the importance of the explicit curriculum in the reproduction of consciousness in capitalistic societies.³⁷ The hidden curriculum also reproduced the attitudes and personality traits upon which work in capitalist society depends.³⁸ Bernstein contended that class membership and family socialization generated distinctive speech patterns in a

---

33. Bowles and Gintis, *Schooling in Capitalist America*.
34. Reich, *Education and the Next Economy*.
35. Bourdieu, "Forms of Cultural Capital."
36. Ibid., 241–58.
37. Apple, *Education and Power*.
38. MacLaren, *Life in Schools*.

Multiculturalism

school classroom. He argued that working-class students learn "restricted" linguistic codes while middle-class children use "elaborated" codes.[39] However, schools generally affirm and reward students who exhibit the elaborately coded middle-class speech while disconfirming and devaluing students who use restricted working-class coded speech. So schools as they are currently structured perpetuate inequalities. Multicultural education dares to challenge the system in the way it is currently structured, demanding that it be made more equitable.

Cultural reproduction theory has critically influenced the field of multicultural education. The incompatibilities or discrepancies between the culture of the school and those of different ethnic and cultural groups have created controversy in making decisions about educational programs and practices that reflect and promote cultural diversity.[40] A positive impact of postmodernism is that we are leaving an age of cultural absolutism for an age of cultural relativism that sees every culture with its own strengths and weaknesses. It validates cultural plurality, allowing educational practices to become more in tune with cultural needs and experiences to meet minority groups where they are, in their own contexts.

Radical Multiculturalism

With the emergence of multiculturalism, educators started to claim that the current schooling failed to integrate diverse racial, cultural, and language backgrounds to enable students to work cooperatively and productively in a school setting.[41] Haddad identified two broad categories of multicultural education: consensus and radical multicultural education.[42] The consensus category positions multicultural education as a reform movement consistent with the American democratic tradition. The goal of multicultural education, therefore, is primarily educational. Educators are called to exert all their influences to unite a divided nation under a common umbrella rather than to create division.

Radical multicultural education, on the other hand, seeks the social and political redistribution of power. Its main curricular goal is the

39. Bernstein, *Class, Codes and Control*.
40. Lee, "Building a Community of Shalom."
41. Banks and McGee Banks, *Multicultural Education*.
42. Haddad, "And Who Is My Neighbor."

development of student social action and empowerment skills.[43] In addition, the primary unit of social analysis is the group (race, gender, class) rather than the individual student.

MULTICULTURALISM AS KIN TO LIBERATION THEOLOGY

Liberation theology in Latin America is basically the effort to relate the teachings of the Christian faith to the lives of the poor and oppressed.[44] It relocates faith from the theoretical and lofty ideals of the mind to the practical everyday experience of the poor and marginalized. Berryman summarizes liberation theology in three points:

1. An interpretation of Christian faith out of the suffering, struggle, and hope of the poor
2. A critique of society and the ideologies sustaining it
3. A critique of the activity of the church and of Christians from the angle of the poor[45]

In the late 1960s liberation theology emerged in Latin America as a self-conscious movement. In 1968 the conference of Latin American bishops held in Medellin, Columbia, focused on the plight of the poor, denouncing the capitalistic monopolies that dominated the society while the masses suffered in abject poverty. They declared:

> It appears to be a time of zeal for full emancipation, of liberation from every form of servitude, of personal maturity and of collective integration. The purpose of liberation theology is to humanize the oppressed by changing the economic, social, and political conditions of life which keep the oppressed in servitude to the oppressor.[46]

Liberation theology includes a number of basic tenets: First, liberation theology has been developed based on an activist agenda for justice-oriented spirituality, along with black theology, which focused on challenging racism in the United States and apartheid in South Africa, and with feminist

---

43. Ibid., 218.
44. Ferm, *Contemporary American Theologies*, 62.
45. Berryman, *Liberation Theology*, 6.
46. Ferm, *Contemporary American Theologies*, 62.

theology, which focused on gender inequalities. Liberation theologians understood Jesus as a liberator who was concerned for the poor and oppressed. Second, liberation theology put the emphasis on Christians' active social and political involvement in order to change society. The purpose of theology is not just concerned with understanding the world, but with changing the world by getting involved directly in the process of liberating the oppressed; a continuing interplay of action and theory intertwined together.[47] In this light, liberation theology shares the same direction as the pedagogy of praxis that Freire initiated. Like Freire, liberation theologians saw the causes of poverty as structural, requiring basic structural change. As pedagogy of praxis suggests, liberation theology claims that such changes come only through political action. Third, education is seen as a critically important intervention to transform society, a process that can enable people to become agents of their own advancement.[48] In order to accomplish this purpose, people should be educated into the fullness of the human condition. In addition, liberation theology believes that Christ freed people to continue the work of creation, which is to become and to build the human community.[49] Hesselgrave and Rommen further state that

> faith can be verified only by doing the truth. Since there is no possibility of establishing a norm for understanding outside of praxis itself, orthopraxis rather than orthodoxy becomes the criterion of sound theology. . . . this understanding of the theological task leads to a Copernican revolution in theology. So, whether we are dealing with a theology of liberation or critical reflection on praxis, it becomes clear that we are dealing with nothing short of a new way of doing theology."[50]

The question arises as to why linking multiculturalism to liberation theology could make it unchristian. To assume that the linkage between multiculturalism and liberation theology is negative is to assume that liberation theology is negative. That assumption implies a denial of an essential core of the gospel of Jesus Christ. Were there socialist influences underlying liberation theology? Well, yes. The question is what those influences are. The idea of equality of all humans is not a secular concept; rather, it is a sacred idea anchored in biblical Christianity.

47. Ibid., 63.
48. Berryman, *Liberation Theology*, 23.
49. Hesselgrave and Rommen, *Contextualization*.
50. Ibid., 95.

Whereas multiculturalism is not a byproduct of liberation theology—as we will soon give a historical analysis of its origin—it is complimentary to liberation theology. The two share some basic ideologies and passions: all persons are created equal, all humans are of equal worth and value, social conditions must not be structured to favor one group to the detriment of others, and the journey towards equality must be organized, intentional, and systematic.

CHAPTER SUMMARY

In this chapter we have examined the various Christian critiques of multiculturalism as having roots in Marxism, postmodernism, and liberation theology. While affirming these roots in certain instances, we have made clear that none of these ideologies embodies the essence of multiculturalism in any meaningful way. Multiculturalism has its own goals and objectives, which cannot be subsumed under the content of these other ideologies. On the contrary, in multiculturalism we see a willingness to take from these ideologies what is humane and just as instruments for advocating for a more cohesive, humane, and just society.

4

The Goals of Multicultural Education

THIS CHAPTER NARROWS THE discourse from multiculturalism as a social movement to multicultural education as a pedagogical principle and movement. This discussion is necessary because our schools have become the context for all forms of social experiments in the last four decades. The idea of multicultural education is central to our discourse because the point has already been made that American schools as they have been historically structured have not been settings for equal educational opportunities, nor have they allowed for diverse educational ideologies and practices outside of the Eurocentric forms that have been transported to this continent.

The idea of multicultural education is seen as a negative concept by some fundamentalist Christians who see the public school as an arena for breeding anti-Christian and anti-European ideologies. This has led to a measureable desertion of the public schools in search of parochial Christian schools and home schooling.

Contrary to the general impression among some conservative Christian groups, multicultural education in schools is not the propagation of homosexual agendas and curriculum. It is not the propagation of Ebonics, nor is it making every child speak Spanish (even though that would be a good thing). Rather, multicultural education addresses major historical factors that have hindered minority children from attaining

> *Multicultural education in schools is not the propagation of homosexual agenda...*

The Goals of Multicultural Education

measurable academic achievements in mainstream American schools for many years.

James Banks articulated the dimensions and development of multicultural education in the United States under five subheadings: Content Integration, Knowledge Construction, Equity Pedagogy, Prejudice Reduction, and Empowering School Culture and Social Structure.[1] Using these five subheadings, we will attempt to clarify the intentions of multicultural education as a worthy social agenda within the American educational setting.

MULTICULTURAL EDUCATION AS CONTENT INTEGRATION IN EDUCATION

Multicultural education attempts to present academic content taught in schools as having multicultural, multiethnic, and global influences. For generations, American schools have taught such subject matters as mathematics, history, and the sciences as ethnocentric subjects. The contributions of individuals not of European descent have been overlooked—and in many cases avoided. The primary numbers we use for mathematical calculations are referred to as Arabic numerals. Where in the K-12 curriculum do we teach American children what we mean by an Arabic numeral, the history and the origin of this numbering system, and the contribution of the Arabic culture to the subject of mathematics? American history has traditionally been the history of America from a Eurocentric perspective. Many history books avoided the acknowledgement that people lived on this continent before the arrival of Columbus. It is an insult to common sense to use such language as ""Columbus found America," or to refer to other Europeans as founding other non-Europeans nations and discovering rivers, falls, and other natural resources, when it was clearly evident that when those Europeans arrived at these places, other people were already there ahead of them.

Content integration demands that we tell the stories and experiences of those earlier people whom the Europeans met at the point of arrival. On the pages of the popular Christian daily devotional, *Our Daily Bread*, the following comments were recently penned:

---

1. Banks, "Teaching for Social Justice, Diversity, and Citizenship."

Multiculturalism

> The Native Americans of Michigan were the state's first highway route engineers. With few exceptions, Michigan's major highways follow the trails they cut through the wilderness hundreds of years before the white man came. A trail was 12–18 inches wide, and for safety the people followed single file. Then pack horses followed these trails, widening them. Later came dirt roads and then the highways.[2]

The same story is true of California where the San Manuel Indians run advertisements reminding Californians that the California highways across San Bernardino County followed old Native American trails. How many American history books contain these facts?

According to Banks, the roots of content integration reach back to the works of an African American scholar, George Washington Williams, whose historical works date back between 1882 and 1883. In his *History of the Negro Race in America From 1619 to 1880*, Williams provided 1,748 pages of historical accounts of the lives and experiences of the Africans who were brought into America. He provided historical facts that would not be found anywhere in the mainstream textbooks of American history. Yet American authors of history books have made no attempts to adapt these new insights to enrich the stories they tell.

Content integration in U.S. history demands that a study of American history embrace all who share the American experience. The American Revolution has for years been a story of the white settlers and their revolts against the oppressive power of the English monarchy. Genuine academic inquiry needs to investigate what the revolution meant for the African Americans who lived under the weight of slavery, who heard the clarion call for liberty and freedom. What did that mean to them? How did they respond to that development? What aspects of the spirit of the Revolution prompted African slaves to show up at the Revolution's call and ask to be recruited to fight for freedom? Secondly, how did the Native Americans view this clarion call for freedom? How did a people who felt that the freedom they had enjoyed for centuries was now being infringed upon by foreign invaders respond to the cry for freedom? American history of the Revolution cannot be full and complete until these stories become part of the whole narrative. Howard Zinn, a white Civil Rights activist, wrote *A People's History of the United States, 1492-Present*. He attempted to capture

---

2. Egner, "Cutting a Trail."

The Goals of Multicultural Education

a holistic view of the American story, yet it is rarely found as a required text in any high school history courses.

Content integration calls for a balance in all fields. The sciences, along with acknowledging the contributions of European males, need to pay attention to and incorporate the contributions of minorities and women to the academic fields. Mathematical practices and activities from around the world should be brought into the conversation as we engage math learning in the schools. When the content of learning is comprehensive and inclusive, all children in our multicultural schools are able to connect with the content materials and not respond to them as foreign subjects. It is important that each group represented in the educational setting see themselves as an integral part of the total curriculum.[3]

MULTICULTURAL EDUCATION AS KNOWLEDGE CONSTRUCTION IN EDUCATION

Knowledge construction refers to the process by which knowledge is constructed or shaped in specific disciplines. The way we interact with reality around us is determined by what we know about that reality. There was a time when we were taught that the earth was flat. How we interacted with the earth, its oceans, and even the sky was shaped almost entirely by the knowledge that the earth was flat. It was not until science disproved that knowledge and handed us an alternate theory that the earth was spherical did we begin to interact with it differently. Knowledge construction first calls into question what we know about reality, especially what we have been taught to believe about people who are different from us. Cultural racism has been both a hidden and open curriculum in the American schools for years. During the earlier years of Eugenics debates, there was open academic dialogue about knowledge constructed so that students see the European cultures and races as superior—and others as inferior. With the demise of the Eugenics era, such knowledge construction became more of a hidden curriculum; with the deliberate efforts to exclude minority issues from the main curriculum and textbooks, students were taught that they were unimportant.[4] Multicultural education now demands that the educational system help construct knowledge that is more respectful of diversity, more unbiased, and more representative of facts, rather than feelings.

    3. Gollnick and Chinn, *Multicultural Education*.
    4. Koppelman and Goodhart, *Understanding Human Differences*.

Multiculturalism

James Banks traced the history of knowledge construction back to the 1960s in the works of revisionist social scientists who were primarily people of color, asking that educational curricular reflect a more balanced view of reality. In 1993, Gary Nash, while not disputing the 1960s historical roots of the knowledge construction movements, indicated that in the 1990s the battle for cultural parity would be fought in the classrooms as African American and other minority parents sought to alter what their children were being taught in schools to include their own experiences, a prediction that has proved to be true in many twenty-first-century American classrooms.[5]

MULTICULTURAL EDUCATION AS EQUITY PEDAGOGY

The idea of equity pedagogy speaks to the need for teachers to apply pedagogical tools and practices that make it possible for all students to learn. Equity pedagogy takes issue with a one-size-fits-all approach to teaching, and instead demands that teaching address the multiple intelligences and diverse ethnic, social, and economic backgrounds of the students. Schooling in America has historically addressed the needs of white middle-class students. Equity pedagogy calls for teachers to go beyond that population and attempt to reach culturally and linguistically diverse students through the tools and strategies they utilize in teaching.

Multicultural education assumes that all children can learn and that all children should be afforded equal educational opportunities to empower them to learn. Equity pedagogy demands that the school systems make intentional efforts to provide every child easy access to knowledge and learning. Children with disabilities are to be educated in the least restrictive environments. This perspective compels the educational system to identify low-performing students and devise tools and strategies that can scaffold learning for them. President George W. Bush in a speech to the NAACP on No Child Left Behind, July 10, 2000, stated, "And I will confront another form of bias: the soft bigotry of low expectations."[6]

> *Multicultural education assumes that all children can learn.*

Equity pedagogy does not mean using the same or similar tools and strategies for all students; rather it means identifying specific tools and strategies

---

5. Nash, "Multiculturalism and History."
6. "Text: George Bush's Speech to the NAACP."

that would be most successful for each population and applying those to ensure their success. Equity is identified as the basic rhetoric of the 1960s, and it provided the basis for both the integrationist movements and the movement towards gender equality in the United States.

MULTICULTURAL EDUCATION AS PREJUDICE REDUCTION

Another goal of multicultural education, according to Banks and McGee Banks, is prejudice reduction. Recognizing the role schools have played over the years in perpetuating ethnic and racial prejudice and inequality, it is only reasonable that the same system that has intentionally and unintentionally perpetuated prejudice becomes intentional in reducing it. School curriculum and organization must be restructured to promote tolerance and appreciation of diversity. Banks and McGee Banks traced the movement towards prejudice reduction as far back as the 1920s when research was conducted on children's racial attitudes with the goal of helping them develop positive attitudes and values towards diversity.[7]

Multicultural education suggests that the educational system can intentionally utilize academic curriculum as well as extracurricular activities to move students beyond tolerance to appreciation and valuing of diversity while reducing a sense of white superiority, which is already created through educational literature, entertainment, and other media that youth are exposed to.[8]

MULTICULTURAL EDUCATION AS EMPOWERING A NEW SCHOOL CULTURE

The idea behind empowering school culture is to restructure the school curriculum and organization so that students from diverse ethnic, socioeconomic, and language backgrounds can feel comfortable and be able to succeed in schools.[9] Such an educational environment does not permit labeling; instead educational disabilities are seen as open doors for addressing specific needs in order to enable students to succeed. The educational cur-

---

7. Banks and McGee Banks, *Handbook of Research*.
8. Koppelman and Goodhart, *Understanding Human Differences*, 174.
9. Banks and McGee Banks, *Handbook of Research*, 6.

riculum and school climate are focused on increasing students' academic achievement, emotional growth, and functionality. The goal is to reach the whole child, with the whole curriculum, in the whole school.

Empowering school culture calls for educational reforms that target students' personal development, academic development, and achievement. This means that teachers are willing to undergo retraining to better serve their students. They are willing to learn new ways of doing things. They improve in their ability to leave their comfort zones to get to know their students and their cultural backgrounds and to connect with them. Administrators are intentional in identifying and employing minority teachers and counselors to better serve students from nonwhite populations and to connect nonwhite students to diverse scholars.

A very strong argument can therefore be made that multicultural education provides a more accurate knowledge base, as it presents more comprehensive and more unbiased content knowledge, contrary to a one-sided culturally biased curriculum.

CHAPTER SUMMARY

This chapter has focused exclusively on multicultural education. We have engaged the idea of multicultural education as content integration, knowledge construction, equity pedagogy, prejudice reduction, and empowering a new school culture.

The chapter has demonstrated the fact that multicultural education aims at producing better-rounded students as it aims at providing students with an enhanced worldview, values, and cultural awareness. While some left-wing activists may find in multicultural education open doors for propagating personal and group views that contradict traditional Christian worldviews, it is important to note that their activities, while a concern, should not be the sole reason for which Christians might reject multiculturalism. We cannot throw away the baby with the bath water; rather, we need to take what is good and reject what is bad.

5

Justice: A Central Idea in Multiculturalism

THE CONCEPT OF SOCIAL justice has almost become an offensive phrase in certain Christian circles. Individuals who claim to be born-again, Bible-believing Christians frown at that phrase and advocate against it and what it stands for. Peter McLaren painted a picture of what he called social justice under siege in America.:

> We inhabit skeptical times, historical moments spawned in a temper of distrust, disillusionment, and despair. Social relations of discomfort and diffidence have always preexisted us but the current historical juncture is particularly invidious in this regard, marked as it is by a rapture of greed, untempered and hypereroticized consumer will, racing currents of narcissism, severe economic and racial injustices, and heightened social paranoia.[1]

While many who benefit from the system as it is at present would like to speak about our free and fair society, failing to acknowledge the fact that for some within this same society the realization of freedom and liberation has become a distant hope rather than a present reality: the immigrant sewing clothes under harsh conditions in a sweatshop, the young boy and girl held as sex slaves in the streets of Detroit and San Francisco, the migrant worker paid less than the minimum wage for a day of back-breaking work under

---

1. McLaren, "Multiculturalism and the Post-modern Critique."

a scorching California sun, and many more. This fact makes it imperative that people of faith critically engage the idea of social justice.

This section will engage the idea of justice—especially social justice—and explore the biblical basis for both ideas of justice and social justice.

A DEFINITION OF JUSTICE

The *Microsoft Encarta College Dictionary* defines justice as "fairness or reasonableness, especially in the way people are treated or decisions are made."[2] Frey contends that justice does not present a "rigorously defined notion," but rather a cluster of normative ideas that are combined in one form or the other.[3] According to him, the idea of justice is contained within the "elementary patterns of every civilization," revealed in every society and place in norms of "distribution and just exchange."[4] Marshall also confronts the challenge of defining justice. According him, "Justice is one of those ideas that combine tremendous emotional potency with a great deal of semantic ambiguity."[5] The *Catholic Encyclopedia* provides a detailed definition we can adopt for the purpose of this work:

> justice is taken in its ordinary and proper sense to signify the most important of the cardinal virtues. It is a moral quality or habit which perfects the will and inclines it to render to each and to all what belongs to them. Of the other cardinal virtues, prudence perfects the intellect and inclines the prudent man to act in all things according to right reason. Fortitude controls the irascible passions; and temperance moderates the appetites according as reason dictates. While fortitude and temperance are self-regarding virtues, justice has reference to others. Together with charity it regulates man's intercourse with his fellow men. But charity leads us to help our neighbor in his need out of our own stores, while justice teaches us to give to another what belongs to him.
>
> Because man is a person, a free and intelligent being, created in the image of God, he has a dignity and a worth vastly superior to the material and animal world by which he is surrounded. Man can know, love, and worship his Creator; he was made for that end, which he can only attain perfectly in the future, immortal,

2. "Justice" *Microsoft Encarta College Dictionary*, 782.
3. Frey, "Impact of the Biblical Idea of Justice," 92.
4. Ibid., 94.
5. Marshall, *Little Book of Biblical Justice*, 4.

and never-ending life to which he is destined. God gave him his faculties and his liberty in order that he might freely work for the accomplishment of his destiny. He is in duty bound to strive to fulfill the designs of his Creator, he must exercise his faculties and conduct his life according to the intentions of his Lord and Master. Because he is under these obligations he is consequently invested with rights, God-given and primordial, antecedent to the State and independent of it. Such are man's natural rights, granted to him by nature herself, sacred, as is their origin, and inviolable. Beside these he may have other rights given him by Church or State, or acquired by his own industry and exertion. All these rights, whatever be their source, are the object of the virtue of justice. Justice requires that all persons should be left in the free enjoyment of all their rights.[6]

This elaborate definition makes certain points that we must take into consideration:

1. Justice is a moral quality that perfects the will and inclines it to render to people their due rights.
2. Justice inclines the person of prudence to act in all situations with respect to right reason.
3. Justice regulates the interactions (intercourse) between persons.
4. Justice teaches us to give to another person what rightfully belongs to him/her.
5. Justice mandates us to allow all persons to enjoy freedom and due process in all situations.

With this understanding of justice as background, let's go a step further to explore the idea of social justice and biblical foundations for social justice.

THE IDEA OF SOCIAL JUSTICE

Social justice has emerged as a popular field of inquiry on which many scholars have written, especially within the context of education and politics. Hytten and Bettez state that while many education scholars have increasingly claimed a social justice orientation to their works, they have often failed to present a clear and precise definition of what they mean by social justice. These researchers examined the idea of social justice from

6. Slater, "Justice."

five different perspectives, among which was a "democratically grounded" perspective. According to them the biggest strength of this perspective "is the holistic vision of justice as a fundamental component of democratic citizenship."[7] Starting with a vision of democracy that balances individual rights and responsibilities, which are also premised upon upholding "the common good," they argue that this perspective makes it possible to see why social justice matters: "Without this vision of justice, democratic life is impossible."[8]

A commonly assumed concept of social justice is fairness. Standish argues that to accept that justice (whether social or otherwise) means fairness is to take a step towards a commitment to equality and accepting that all humans are equal.[9] In light of this and the preceding arguments, let's underscore certain facts in our attempt to define social justice:

1. The idea of social justice assumes justice in a social setting, which means justice as administered within a community of human beings. This community could be homogeneous or heterogeneous, but social justice points to the idea of a commitment to equal treatment of all human beings under a given set of laws in a social setting.

2. The idea of social setting points to the variety of political, religious, cultural, and philosophical orders that have defined human environments from the point of human existence.[10]

Thus, social justice points to the administration of justice and fairness in these settings in given times and places. In twenty-first-century United States, therefore, the idea of social justice must be seen as the administration of fairness and justice across all the political, religious, cultural, educational, and philosophical spheres that exist in contemporary society. It points to a deliberate, equitable, and uniform administration and adherence to the rights of all citizens to life, liberty, and the pursuit of happiness. Gardner and Toope, in their research on a strengths-based approach to social justice, proposed that social justice within the educational setting should involve four things, among many others: "recognizing students in context, critically engaging strengths and positivity, nurturing democratic

---

7. Hytten and Bettez, "Understanding Education for Social Justice," 20.
8. Ibid.
9. Standish, "Social Justice in Translation."
10. Cuzzort and King, *Humanity and Modern Social Thought*.

Justice: A Central Idea in Multiculturalism

relations, and enacting creative and flexible pedagogies."[11] A critical analysis of these four considerations reveal that none of them would be considered diametrically opposed to any Christian principle, but rather, all four would very much find biblical validations.

BIBLICAL FOUNDATIONS FOR SOCIAL JUSTICE

The Hebrew word for justice is *mishpat*. Right from the creation story we note that justice is at the heart of God.[12] God's desire for the world from the creation of mankind was the establishment of a just society. The purpose for which he separated Abraham from his people was so he could start with him the making of a new people who would operate in justice and righteousness, a constant Old Testament theme. In the laws of Moses God made clear his eternal commitment to the establishment of a just society made up of his own people, God's treasured possession (Exod 19:5). It can be argued that the books of the Law (the Pentateuch) chronicled God's standards of justice beginning with Abraham and Sarah's dealings with Hagar, an Egyptian slave girl, through the delivery of the commandments at Sinai, into the details of the law as chronicled in Numbers, Deuteronomy, and Joshua.

> *Justice is at the heart of God.*

The books of the Chronicles of the Kings of Israel and Judah have a recurring theme of justice and fair play. The king was supposed to be God's representative in administering justice. Quite often the kings failed to duly represent God in this regard, and God would make his disapproval of their conduct clear. This is evident when God sent the prophet Nathan to confront David concerning his personal injustices to the house of Uriah. The prophets of God emerged over time as the paramount defenders of the interests of the poor and the less privileged. In the encounter between Ahab and Naboth (1 Kgs 21), the prophet Elijah invited himself into the case, taking the side of Naboth against the king and his wife. In so doing, he clearly portrayed the fact that God has continuously taken sides with the weak and powerless over and against the strong and powerful; the poor and less privileged over the rich and well connected. The fight for social justice

---

11. Gardner and Toope, "A Social Justice Perspective on Strengths-based Approaches," 88.

12. McIlroy, *A Biblical View of Law and Justice*, 89.

can be said to be a prerogative of God himself, who through biblical history demonstrated it through his prophets.

The institution of the Old Testament prophetic ministry that aimed at justice and righteousness best exemplifies this call for social justice. The prophet was God's mouthpiece in confronting the evil of the society and holding the rulers to the principles of law, order, and justice. They were singled out for the duty of calling God's people back to his covenant with them and challenging the kings, priests, and rulers not only to obey, but also to enforce the laws of God by a pursuit of justice.[13]

The prophet Amos stands out among his peers in this pursuit of social justice. In his cry for justice Amos denounced a plethora of ills: exploitation and suppression of the weak, extracting levies and taxes, selling the righteous and the poor into slavery, economic cheating and exploitation, pursuit of excessive profits, sexual immorality, corrupt judicial systems, bribery, addiction to luxury, and so on.[14] Amos stood tall among his peers in condemning social injustices of every kind. His message is summed up by Doorly: "Yahweh is a God of justice who rejects even the people who claim him as their God when these people destroy the fabric of their society by oppressing their fellows."[15] The prophet Ezekiel was even more forthright,

> Therefore this is what the Sovereign Lord says to them: See, I myself will judge between the fat sheep and the lean sheep. Because you shove with flank and shoulder, butting all the weak sheep with your horns until you have driven them away, I will save my flock, and they will no longer be plundered. I will judge between one sheep and another. I will place over them one shepherd, my servant David, and he will tend them; he will tend them and be their shepherd. I the Lord will be their God, and my servant David will be prince among them. I the Lord have spoken. (34:20–24)

The idea of social justice, therefore, should not be offensive to those who claim the God of Amos and Ezekiel as their God. True worshippers of Yahweh must become his allies in rooting out evil and enthroning justice and righteousness. Doorly went further to argue,

> It may be that some of the voices critical of our culture are crying out the truth of Yahweh to us. We have been unfair . . . we have discriminated against groups of our own citizens, structuring into

13. Ibid., 90.
14. Hasel, *Understanding the Book of Amos*.
15. Doorly, *Prophet of Justice*, 72.

Justice: A Central Idea in Multiculturalism

our own culture discriminatory and oppressive practices which cause many of our own citizens to lead marginal existences. There is a deadening despair concentrated unfairly in many identifiable groups of people, both in our nation and throughout the world today. Their position in society assuring for them lives of frustration, pain and anger, is not different from the plight of many Israelites in the days of Amos.[16]

This truth, though painful and shaming, must be confronted, and this is what the idea of multiculturalism is doing in our society today. Generations of institutionalized discrimination, deprivation, dehumanization, and marginalization must be confronted. Justice must flow down like mighty waters across this land that claims Yahweh as her God. This justice is not only social in its dimensions, but it is spiritual and moral also. We cannot escape its call.

Marshall articulated five foundations of justice in the biblical history as Shalom, Covenant, Torah, Deed-Consequence, and Atonement. According to him, the idea of shalom assumes the presence of justice and peace. He argues that there can be no peace without justice.[17] Biblical justice, he argues, "requires an activist response to evil, a radical intervention to 'loose the bonds of injustice, to undo the thongs of the yoke, to let the oppressed go free, and to break every yoke'" (Isa 58:6).[18] This is what social justice is all about. Social justice is at the heart of God.

> *Justice demands that generations of institutionalized discrimination, deprivation, dehumanization, and marginalization must be confronted.*

In the New Testament, the Greek word *dikaiosyne* conveys the idea of justice. The call to social justice is just as loud and clear in the New Testament as in the Old Testament. Multiple New Testament passages call attention to this mandate:

1. Matthew 7:12 — Christ advocates fair play.
2. Matthew 23:23 — Neglect of justice is denounced.
3. Luke 6:23 — Justice is doing to others as you would have them do unto you.

---

16. Ibid., 73.
17. Marshall, *Little Book of Biblical Justice*, 13.
18. Ibid., 33.

Multiculturalism

4. Luke 11:42		Neglect of justice is denounced.
5. James 1:27		Justice is defined as acceptable religion.
6. James 2:1–8		A very broad definition of injustice is provided and condemned.
7. James 2:14–17		Faith without works of justice is defined as dead faith.

In his earthly ministry, Jesus proved himself to be a relentless advocate for social justice. In Luke 4 when he declared his manifesto before his townsfolk in Galilee, he stated among other things, that he was anointed "to proclaim freedom for the prisoners and recovery of sight for the blind, to set the oppressed free." His agenda included a social justice bias. Commenting on Jesus' ministry of fostering justice and fair play, Nardoni writes, "according to Luke, Jesus is God's anointed, endowed with the power of the Spirit, sent as the messianic king to proclaim the good news of liberation and to implement it through words and deeds."[19] Wow! To see Jesus as committed to the liberation movement may sound socialist to some, but indeed he was. He not only cared for the spiritual conditions of people, he cared for their physical (the lame, the blind, the deaf, and the dumb), social (Zacchaeus, the Samaritan woman) and moral liberation (the woman caught in adultery). Nardoni further argues that the idea of justice in the Lukan account envisions "a new map of relationships, where there is a place for any person who believes in the gospel, without any discrimination based on race, nationality, sex, social status, or religious tradition."[20]

Maybe a biblical concept of social justice is better summarized in the messianic prophecies of the prophet Isaiah:

> Here is my servant, whom I uphold,
> my chosen one in whom I delight;
>
> I will put my Spirit on him,
> and he will bring justice to the nations.
>
> He will not shout or cry out,
> or raise his voice in the streets.
>
> A bruised reed he will not break,
> and a smoldering wick he will not snuff out.

---

19. Nardoni, *Rise Up, O Judge*, 259.
20. Ibid., 259.

> In faithfulness he will bring forth justice;
> he will not falter or be discouraged
>
> till he establishes justice on earth.
> In his teaching the islands will put their hope. (42:1–4)

The gospel of Christ dismantled the most powerful and unjust society of Rome by the power of the word: not with the sword or the bow and arrow. The biblical call to social justice is not a call to violence; rather it is a call to righteousness, peace, fairness, and the fear of God. When God's people rise and take a stand against evil and injustices in their midst, the most powerful and most violent of forces of darkness will be brought to their knees.

CHAPTER SUMMARY

In this chapter we have taken time to define the idea of justice and social justice. We have appealed to biblical history to show that the idea of justice and fair play begins with the Old Testament laws and runs through the prophetic ministries of the Old Testament prophets and up to the ministry of Christ himself. We have established that justice and social justice are at the heart of God.

Based on this assumption, the church of God is called to take sides with their God in fighting for the freedom of captives, release of prisoners, and recovery for the disenfranchised. This chapter, above all else, makes clear that God has already taken a side on the fight for justice, and his side is with the weak and oppressed, not the powerful and the oppressor.

6

Biblical Foundations for Multiculturalism

MULTICULTURALISM IS GOD'S CREATION. To assume that God created the universe including this planet earth and at the same time suppose that cultural and human diversity originated outside of his plan and purpose is to assume that multiculturalism originated outside of God's sphere of influence or that it was a creative error on the part of God. The pages of Scripture provide abundant proof that our God is responsible for and favors human diversity. To fully appreciate this insight we will examine what it means that humans were created in the image of God. We will examine God's covenants with humanity starting with Noah, the ideas of God's mission, God's kingdom, and God's people as they bear upon human diversity and multiculturalism.

CREATION IN IMAGO DEI

The very first creation account recorded in the book of Genesis states that God created humankind in his own image:

> Then God said, "Let us make mankind in our image, in our likeness, so that they may rule over the fish in the sea and the birds in the sky, over the livestock and all the wild animals, and over all the creatures that move along the ground." So God created mankind

Biblical Foundations for Multiculturalism

in his own image, in the image of God he created them; male and female he created them.

A careful examination of this narrative points to both unity and diversity as part of God's original plan for humankind. Although this passage does not present any indication of ethnic diversity, since God created humanity as one human race, it prominently features gender diversity.

What then does it mean that mankind was created in the image of God? This question has occupied theologians, sages, and poets. What about our mortal flesh, which is no different from that of the beasts of the field—is that flesh created in the image of God? Modern scientists have seen so many similarities between humans and the beasts so that they have concluded we are higher animals, giving up on the possibility of a divinity within us. Considering the fact that God is spirit and we are humans, one can argue that his image in us could not possibly be in our physical forms and features. Our forms and features are normative for earthly existence and would not serve the divine deity very well. As humans we historically visualized God as one of us, assigning to him features like our eyes, mouth, legs, hands, etc. (Isa 59:1–2). The whole idea of God as an anthropomorphism is just a result of our inability as humans to conceptualize him as he is, so we paint him in our own image and begin to imagine that he shares some of our own attributes. Glasser and colleagues write about the description of God: "Genesis begins with God but offers no description of him. Although the whole Old Testament is about God, it will tell us nothing of what he is like in himself."[1]

That we were made in his image has little or nothing do to with God sharing our physical forms; rather, we are the ones who have been allowed to share a little of his attributes. Matthew Henry's *Bible Commentary* paints this picture:

> Man was to be a creature different from all that had been hitherto made. Flesh and spirit, heaven and earth, must be put together in him. God said, "Let us make man." Man, when he was made, was to glorify the Father, Son, and Holy Ghost. Into that great name we are baptized, for to that great name we owe our being. It is the soul of man that especially bears God's image. Man was made upright, Ec 7:29. His understanding saw Divine things clearly and

---

1. Glasser, et al., *Announcing the Kingdom*, 30.

Multiculturalism

> truly; there were no errors or mistakes in his knowledge; his will consented at once, and in all things, to the will of God.[2]

If we subscribe to the commentary above, that it is the soul of man that bears the image of God, then it means that every person with a soul—which is the essential distinguishing factor between humans and animals—was created in the image of God. If this assumption holds water, then all humans, regardless of their shade of skin, were made in God's image. We would not find many evangelical Christians who would disagree with this conclusion. The problem, however, is that many Western evangelicals—while not questioning this theological truth—have comfortably pushed it to the background and bought into a non-Christian concept of humanity that divides us up along ethnic and racial lines. Concerning this problem, Ken Ham and Charles Ware write,

> There still persist an "us versus them" mentality and the vast majority of churches are still segregated. Much of the fundamental/evangelical church still struggles with trusting relationships. Despite the proper biblical teaching of humanity's unity in the first Adam and Christians' unity in the Last Adam, we still see too few authentic relationships cross ethnic lines.[3]

Whereas science has proved time and time again that our human differences are only skin deep, we have gotten stuck in our old ideologies and theories of the human race handed down to us from the Eugenics era. Some American evangelicals are unable to imagine that they may be worshipping a Jewish savior with the Bedouin-like physical features of a first-century Palestinian; they insist on the picture of a blond Christ with white skin and hazel eyes. That was not the image of God to which the writer of Genesis refers. That's actually making God in our own image.

David Burnett identified certain characteristics that distinguish humans from other creatures of God, which he believes point to the image of God that we bear:

1. Relationality: We were created with the capability to have a relationship with God and with one another.

2. Personality: We were created in God's image to manifest his nature and character in individual personhood.

---

2. *Matthew Henry's Bible Commentary*, vol. 1: *Genesis to Deuteronomy*, 8.
3. Ham and Ware, *One Race, One Blood*, 57.

Biblical Foundations for Multiculturalism

3. Creativity: We were endowed with the ability to create and reform our environment, and often altar it significantly.
4. Immortality: Burnett argues that we were created to last eternally. Death came in only as a result of the Fall. One can take the liberty to add the fact that our human soul was not made to die, hence our immortality.[4]

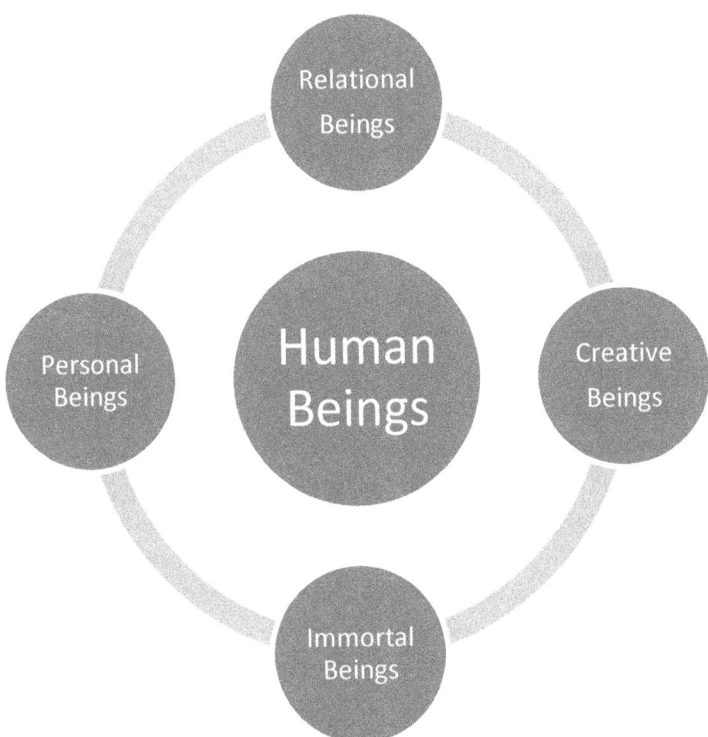

Figure 6.1: Burnett's Human Characteristics

Burnett points out that a prominent idea in the *imago Dei* concept is the idea of a common ancestry of humankind (Acts 17:26).

All of humanity shares a common ancestry in God our maker. He made us in his image, allowing us to share the same perishable substance of dust. Whereas other environmental and evolutionary factors may explain the variations in our pigmentation, our souls reflect the image of God

---

4. Burnett, *Healing of the Nations*, 24.

without any variation. Our souls are susceptible to both good and evil regardless of the tone of our skin. All of our souls are able to be saved through the grace of God if only we can believe and allow Christ to come in and take his place. The soul is a feature we share with no other creature of God. That is the very fact that makes us special.

Richard Willis sees the racial assumptions that have led to racial preferences, prejudices, and segregation as contradictory to a biblical understanding of *imago Dei*.[5] According to him, affirmation of racial segregation, prejudice, and preferences affirms only the dignity of some of God's children and not of others. It denies the humanity of one person while upholding the humanity of another. A logical pursuit of Willis' view reveals that such a position is both unchristian and unbiblical. It not only rejects the wisdom and grace of God at creation, but also questions his power and authority to set the rules for human relationships.

Reflecting on Martin Luther King Jr.'s theology in the Civil Rights movement, Willis states that considering the fact that the U.S. Constitution and the Declaration of Independence did not take into consideration the plight of the African American, King had to interpret his call for freedom through theological lenses. To effectively do that he had to appeal to the efficacy of *imago Dei*. Willis argues that in King's embrace of the *imago Dei* as the basis for affirming one's place in the world, he intended to "refute the myths of racial inferiority, thereby providing a historically oppressed people with the psychological ability to move beyond centuries of oppressive socialization bent toward the creation of an impotent labor force."[6] According to Willis, King saw *imago Dei* as a universal condition that interrelates all humanity at its most basic level.

In the First Adam, therefore, all humanity regardless of race and ethnicity was formed and born into sin. In the Last Adam all of humanity was redeemed and restored into fellowship with God. So the New Testament church is the only human institution that can boast of a true humanity that reflects *imago Dei* in its pure sense. That is only possible if that church is indeed a church in the true sense of the word.

> *In the Last Adam all of humanity was redeemed and restored into fellowship with God.*

Biblical insights from *imago Dei* therefore provide a solid foundation for

---

5. Willis, *Martin Luther King, Jr.*, 24–25.
6. Ibid., 116.

appreciating cultural diversity within the body of Christ. Arthur Glasser and colleagues write, "On the basis of the Genesis account no people or race should regard itself as superior in origin or essence."[7] They quote Walter Eichrodt: "As mankind appears at the beginning of Israel's records as a single entity, so too, in Israel's view of the future, mankind appears as the united Community of nations receiving God's new world, and thus returning to their origin."[8] Glasser and colleagues see Babel as demonstrating humanity's refusal to obey God. The building of the tower is seen as indicating "insecurity, vanity, and self-centeredness." It points to human arrogance and the tendency to create a universally homogeneous human kingdom. Human diversity and ethnic plurality are seen as resulting from God's punishment of human disobedience and sinfulness. Viewed through this perspective, diversity becomes a punishment resulting from sin.

These writers, however, see a positive aspect of human diversity. At Babel, the God who had promised Noah he was not going to destroy the whole human race put into motion a process by which humanity could not find unity outside of his will and purpose for them. While separated by ethnicity, language, and culture, humanity is able to come together as one under the power of the Holy Spirit as a people belonging to the kingdom of God.[9] They write, "At Babel God was deeply involved in fracturing the human race, shattering its unity, and scattering people over the face of the earth, even though this was also an act of grace in preserving the lives of those present at Babel."[10]

It must be acknowledged here that anthropologists have a different explanation for cultural diversity. They have traced our linguistic and cultural diversity to evolutionary trends that naturally occur as humans develop. They assert that the variations in our environments affect the way we adapt to the environment and over time those adaptations become essential cultural traits that distinguish us from other human groups.[11] Over time, human groups develop culture-specific modes for organizing knowledge, thought, and communication. To fit into such a society, children and newcomers have to be acculturated into that social group.[12] Anthropological

---

7. Glasser et al., *Announcing the Kingdom*, 36.
8. Eichrodt, *Man in the Old Testament*, 36.
9. Glasser et al., *Announcing the Kingdom*, 52.
10. Ibid., 53.
11. Burnett, *Healing of the Nations*, 40.
12. Minanmi and Ovando, "Language Issues in Multicultural Contexts," 573.

views, however, are very limited. They are simply human attempts to explain what is otherwise beyond our ability to explain. Niebuhr states that human history, though rooted in the natural process, is much more than "the determined sequences of natural causation or the capricious variations and occurrences of the natural world."[13] So to explain human diversity from a purely scientific or anthropological perspective is to ascribe to human knowledge much more credibility than it has earned.

The unity celebrated in the church differs from the events at Babel. Babel was a human attempt to create for themselves a homogenous kingdom. Contrary to God's blessing to Noah and his descendants—"As for you, be fruitful and increase in number; multiply on the earth and increase upon it" (Gen 9:7)—the generation after Noah decided to create their own history. The Scripture says,

> Now the whole world had one language and a common speech. As people moved eastward, they found a plain in Shinar and settled there. They said to each other, "Come, let's make bricks and bake them thoroughly." They used brick instead of stone, and tar for mortar. Then they said, "Come, let us build ourselves a city, with a tower that reaches to the heavens, so that we may make a name for ourselves; otherwise we will be scattered over the face of the whole earth. (Gen 11:1–4)

Speech and language are the basic vehicles for social interaction and cultural identity. A common human language and culture evidently made humans self-centered rather than God-centered. Rather than pursue and fulfill God's purpose for mankind, they carved out for themselves a purpose: "to make a name for ourselves." This is the heart of all the ills of ethnocentrism, racial or ethnic bigotry, and prejudice. When a race of humans begins to see so much value in their cultural identity that it overshadows God's purpose for them, they must be living at Babel. God has only one plan for those who live in Babel, to scatter them. For those who seek comfort in ethnically or racially segregated communities, God's promise to you is confusion and dispersion. That structure is contrary to God's plan for humanity, and all who hold on to their segregated structure work against the will of God. Arthur Glasser et al. present some lessons we must learn from Babel:

1. There is a limit to God's grace: God is never indifferent to sin and sinfulness. Time may pass, but God will definitely punish sinfulness.

---

13. Niebuhr, *Nature and Destiny of Man*, 1.

2. God's mission is paramount: At Babel, God was at work to fracture and shatter the unity of the human race so as to preserve them, and ultimately make them his own people.

3. It is human to desire to make a name, but be careful: Babel warns against the idolatrous exaltation of self and the possibility of hostility towards others.

4. God punishes disobedience: The descendants of Noah did not seem to have learned from the recent history of their ancestors. God's people need to learn from history.[14]

Multiculturalism therefore should not become a threat or be treated as a threat to the body of Christ, but rather as an opportunity to be embraced, for any ecclesiastical body that embraces a diverse human population represents the kingdom in its true and pure sense. An ecclesiastical structure that opposes multiculturalism either has failed to clearly understand the plan of God for humanity, the nature of the kingdom, or still operates from its sin nature.

COVENANT AND THE CONCEPT OF GOD'S CALL

Biblical history reveals that the God of the Old and New Testaments was and is a relational God. Traditional Christian church doctrines have established over time that humanity was created to be in fellowship with God. The story of the pre-Fall Eden is a story of God who comes down in the cool of the day to fellowship with humanity, the works of his hand. With such a fellowship broken at the Fall, humanity tended to turn away from God. The Bible records that

> the Lord saw how great the wickedness of the human race had become on the earth, and that every inclination of the thoughts of the human heart was only evil all the time. The Lord regretted that he had made human beings on the earth, and his heart was deeply troubled. (Gen 6:5–6)

In this encounter God looked down at the human race—one human race that had departed from his plans for it and embraced wickedness—and God regretted making mankind. This could be said to be the height of a cosmic battle between the forces of evil and good. Satan was intent on derailing

---

14. Glasser et al., *Announcing the Kingdom*, 52–53.

Multiculturalism

the plan of God as he launched his assault on the souls of men. God, who is holy and righteous, would not put up with such extreme perversion and so his justice came into play. God must cleanse the earth of this extreme wickedness:

> So the Lord said, "I will wipe from the face of the earth the human race I have created—and with them the animals, the birds and the creatures that move along the ground—for I regret that I have made them." (Gen 6:7)

While God's justice was at work to cleanse the earth of the wickedness of people, his grace was also at work to make a way of escape for fallen humanity. Since humanity as a group has fallen so short, God's grace looked for one man, who could become the link between humanity and God's grace. The Scripture says, "But Noah found favor in the eyes of the Lord" (Gen 6:8).

To understand the idea of covenant we must engage a characterization from Glasser et al. of the biblical account of human history as universal and particular.[15] According to them, universal history characterizes the period of biblical history when the unity of the human race is most pronounced: at creation, the Fall, judgment, and dispersion at Babel. At creation one human race was created. At the Fall, humanity fell as one. At judgment (Gen 6–8) God judged humanity as one. Even in the covenant with Noah, God was still dealing with humanity as one, for the promises God made to Noah were for all of humanity. In the dispersion at Babel he dealt with humanity as one. Glasser et al. write, "No person escaped God's language-related judgment arising from the rebellious attempt to oppose God at Babel."[16] "Particular History" is characterized as beginning in Genesis chapter 12, when God called Abram and decided to make out of him a new people that would become his own people. So from Noah to Abraham, to Israel, to the church, there is a plan and purpose that transcends those individuals and groups towards God's plan for humanity as a whole to make a people for himself.

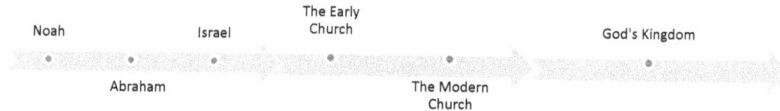

Figure 7.1: The Making of God's People

---

15. Ibid., 29.
16. Ibid.

Biblical Foundations for Multiculturalism

According to Glasser and coauthors, the second period of human history began with Abram and concludes in "Jesus' redemptive death, burial, resurrection, and ascension." With the coming of the Holy Spirit, the birth of the church—the new people of God—a new universal history was launched in which the idea of God's people once again embraces humanity from all ends of the earth. This framework from Glasser et al. will guide our attempt to engage the concept of God's people within the idea of a covenant relationship.

God's Covenant with Noah

Concerning God's covenant with Noah following the flood, the Bible states:

> Then God blessed Noah and his sons, saying to them, "Be fruitful and increase in number and fill the earth. The fear and dread of you will fall on all the beasts of the earth, and on all the birds in the sky, on every creature that moves along the ground, and on all the fish in the sea; they are given into your hands. Everything that lives and moves about will be food for you. Just as I gave you the green plants, I now give you everything.

"But you must not eat meat that has its lifeblood still in it. And for your lifeblood I will surely demand an accounting. I will demand an accounting from every animal. And from each human being, too, I will demand an accounting for the life of another human being.

> "Whoever sheds human blood,
> by humans shall their blood be shed;
>
> for in the image of God
> has God made mankind.
>
> As for you, be fruitful and increase in number; multiply on the earth and increase upon it."
>
> Then God said to Noah and to his sons with him: "I now establish my covenant with you and with your descendants after you and with every living creature that was with you—the birds, the livestock and all the wild animals, all those that came out of the ark with you—every living creature on earth. I establish my covenant with you: Never again will all life be destroyed by the waters of a flood; never again will there be a flood to destroy the earth."
> And God said, "This is the sign of the covenant I am making between me and you and every living creature with you, a covenant

> for all generations to come: I have set my rainbow in the clouds, and it will be the sign of the covenant between me and the earth. Whenever I bring clouds over the earth and the rainbow appears in the clouds, I will remember my covenant between me and you and all living creatures of every kind. Never again will the waters become a flood to destroy all life. Whenever the rainbow appears in the clouds, I will see it and remember the everlasting covenant between God and all living creatures of every kind on the earth."
>
> So God said to Noah, "This is the sign of the covenant I have established between me and all life on the earth." (Gen 9:1–17)

This covenant is the first in recorded biblical history. God enters into a covenant with humanity as one race. Whereas Noah and his descendants were the only survivors among mankind, the covenant was nevertheless with humanity as a single entity, not just Noah and his descendants. This was God giving humanity a second chance through his grace. The universality of the covenant is obvious as God makes mankind head over the beasts of the field and gives mankind all species of animals, plants, and fish as food.

It is also important to note that this covenant was not exclusively with humanity, but embraced all living things. God said he was making this covenant with all living things that were with Noah in the ark and that he would never again destroy the earth by flood. In this covenant we not only encounter our common humanity, we also encounter our common purpose with the rest of creation. Not many other biblical passages confront us with God's interest in the preservation of the ecosystem and all living things as does this passage. So in this covenant we go beyond multiculturalism to ecological responsibility and environmental preservation. God, even our God, made a covenant with the birds of the air and the beasts of the field to preserve them.

So in the Noahic covenant, God promised the preservation and protection of all humanity. Those humans who now live in the draught-ridden East African plains, those in Los Angeles's Skid Row, and those in Mexico City's and Calcutta's ghettos have all been given a promise of preservation and protection by the Almighty. All of God's people entered into a covenant relationship with God in Noah. That is why his rain falls on the wicked as well as the righteous (Matt 5:48). No one human person was excluded from that covenant of protection and preservation. Therefore, when God's people engage in the task of protecting the weak, feeding the hungry, and fighting for the emancipation of the enslaved, we become allies with God in this work of protection and preservation. This is the heart of social justice.

God's Covenant with Abraham

In Abraham we see God's choice of one man from among all the peoples of the earth. The Bible does not point to any prerequisite quality or qualification that positioned Abraham for this special favor. We are not told what personal attributes or characteristics qualified Abraham for this honor. Rather, we read that this was one man from a lineage of men who left Ur of the Chaldeans and ended up settling in Haran. Then Scripture reads,

> The Lord had said to Abram; "Go from your country, your people and your father's household to the land I will show you. I will make you into a great nation, and I will bless you; I will make your name great, and you will be a blessing. I will bless those who bless you, and whoever curses you I will curse; and all peoples on earth will be blessed through you." (Gen 12:1–3)

God initiated this relationship. God made the promises and Abram was only a recipient of God's grace. God's call of Abram was quickly accompanied by promises that culminated in a covenant relationship. As the scriptural account goes, Abram responded to these promises in obedience and left Haran for the land of Canaan. Abram's leaving Haran and heading down to Canaan in obedience to God was credited to Abraham as righteousness.

God's choice of Abram confronts us with God's rejection of the other members of his family, his ethnicity, his country, and his entire generation. In the covenant with him, we encounter a move in which—outside of the scope of the universal covenant with Noah and all mankind—God now elects to choose a particular people from among the human race, with whom he would cut his covenant. The choice of Abram and the rejection his kinsmen points to the fact that this call was not necessarily a call to an ethnic group or cultural group; rather, it was a personal call. It was not the call of a people, but the call of a person. The extension of the covenant to his descendants after him was still not an ethnic or cultural privilege, but a privilege based on personal relationship with God. The choice of Isaac contrasts with the rejection of Ishmael. The choice of Jacob contrasts with the rejection of Esau. So we see that it is not about ethnicity, race, or lineage. It is about a relationship. It is noteworthy that when God asked Abram to leave his family and country to go to a place, the place was described as a land that I will show you. It was not until he arrived in that land in obedience to God that God told him he would give him that land as an inheritance for him and his descendants after him. Glasser et al., analyzing God's covenant with Israel had this to say,

> This dual act, election and covenant, can be comprehended only in terms of his *ahaba* (his election-love) and his *hesed* (his covenant-love). . . . God existed before Israel because he willed to do so (Deut. 7:6–8). . . . God existed before Israel, meaning that if he once existed without them, he could do so again.[17]

One can argue here that God's choice of Abram was not necessarily about Abram as much as it was about God. God had a plan for mankind, and he chose Abram as the instrument through which he could carry out that plan. What is paramount here is not Abram's qualities and spiritual prowess, but rather God's love and kindness (*hesed*), in which he would choose to carry out his sovereign will through frail and sinful humanity. In Abraham, God launched the particular history, in which he chose to no longer deal with humanity as a unit but to call human beings to himself as individuals. According to Lasor, Hubbard, and Bush, "Although Abraham still moved in the religious milieu of his day, his departure for Canaan at God's bidding was also a departure from his polytheistic past to a single-minded devotion to the one God who revealed himself to him."[18] This personal response and personal devotion lies at the heart of this new covenant relationship. The election and covenant are not rights; rather, they are privileges that God bestowed upon Abraham and his descendants.

At the core of America's racism and feelings of racial superiority is the idea of manifest destiny, according which Americans have often seen themselves as chosen by God at the exclusion of other peoples, given a land of such beauty and resources, and preserved through adversities to establish a great nation. A sad reality is that this idea of manifest destiny is more prominent among Bible-believing Christians who should know better. Despite his close walk with God and the fact that God had already promised to deliver the land of Canaan to him and his descendants, Abraham exhibited a high degree of sensitivity to his Canaanite neighbors. Abraham maintained a separation from Canaanites, having left their polytheistic and idolatrous ways and entered a new relationship with God. He continuously saw himself as "an alien and a stranger among" them (Gen 23:4). The

---

17. Ibid., 57.
18. Lasor, Hubbard, and Bush, *Old Testament Survey*, 110.

Canaanites, however, saw him as "a mighty prince among us" (Gen 23:6), a testament to Abraham's witness and sensitivity in dealing with them. Oh, that God's people would live among the unbelievers in humility and gentleness as aliens and strangers in this world! For then they would see us as mighty princes and princesses.

> *At the core of America's racism and feelings of racial superiority is the idea of manifest destiny.*

The covenant with Abraham was not designed to create an ethnocentric and arrogant race, but to make a special people of God, through whom "all peoples on earth will be blessed" (Gen 12:3). In Genesis 15 God established this covenant in the manner of a Hittite ritual covenant relationship, with which Abraham was familiar. In walking through the halves of the sacrifice and symbolically stepping on the blood of the covenant, God bound himself in oath to his own portion of the covenant relationship. In this very act God made clear his identity as a personal God, not just a universal God. He is a God who enters into covenant with his people. He called Abraham in an "I-Thou" encounter, and Abraham responded to him as a person, not an idea, or concept, or location.

In that covenant, Abraham and God made commitments to each other as two personal beings, each bound by the same covenant to fulfill their individual obligations. It is significant to note that this covenant was neither ethnic nor national. Abraham had many sons, among whom were Ishmael and the seven sons of Keturah, yet only through Isaac would the covenant continue. Isaac had two sons, Esau and Jacob, yet only through Jacob would the covenant continue. Personal relationship and response to God become a primary qualifier for being in this covenant relationship.

Let no Christian think that one's ethnicity or race qualifies a person for the call of God. Let no one think that family history and parental spirituality makes a way for this glorious call. The prophet Ezekiel painted the picture rather graphically: "'The parents eat sour grapes, and the children's teeth are set on edge?' As surely as I live, declares the Sovereign Lord, you will no longer quote this proverb in Israel" (Ezek 18:2–3). He goes further to say,

> The one who sins is the one who will die. The child will not share the guilt of the parent, nor will the parent share the guilt of the child. The righteousness of the righteous will be credited to them,

and the wickedness of the wicked will be charged against them. (Ezek 18:20)

Faith is a personal responsibility, not an ethnic or national identity. God's people must quit hanging on to national and ethnic identities as though it is their passport to heaven.

God's Covenant with Israel

Whereas God's covenant with Abraham began and ended with God's election, invitation, and promises, the covenant with Israel began on a different note. Here was a generation that was supposed to know about God's covenant with Abraham, but they did not. When Moses was asked to go to them he asked the question, "Suppose I go to the Israelites and say to them, 'The God of your fathers has sent me to you,' and they ask me, 'What is his name?'" (Exod 3:13). Here was a generation that was supposed to have a personal relationship with God, but they did not. They had just recently given up the gods of the Egyptians that they worshipped during their time in Egypt. Now that God had acted decisively and delivered them from the yoke of their slave masters, after he had revealed himself to them as the God of their fathers, Abraham, Isaac, and Jacob, God invited them into a personal relationship with him. The events at Mount Sinai, recorded in Exodus 19 and 20, were both national and personal in nature. Whereas God invited Israel to meet him at the mountain as one people, he invited them to individually consecrate themselves for that encounter. The call to a people known as Israel is of no consequence unless the individuals who make up that nation have each responded to God at a personal level.

At Mount Sinai God initiated a covenant with Israel with a conditional clause as the preamble: "Now if you obey me fully and keep my covenant, then out of all nations you will be my treasured possession. . . . you will be for me a kingdom of priests and a holy nation" (Exod 19:5–6). Note the "if . . . then . . ." clause. When Moses recounted the words of this covenant to Israel and told them what God was requiring of them, they responded together, "We will do everything the Lord has said" (v. 8). Consequently God gave Moses and the people of Israel the Ten Commandments, the code of ethics that should inform this obedience they had just pledged. In Exodus 24 the covenant is ratified with blood sprinkled on the people. Writing about the personal nature of this covenant, Hubbard and colleagues state, "The treaty was written in very personal terms, using 'I-Thou' dialogue

Biblical Foundations for Multiculturalism

pattern."[19] Whereas Israel was called as one people, the terms of the covenant was binding on them as individuals. The Ten Commandments focused on individual personal conduct in the "I-Thou" relationship with God and in the "I-Thou" relationships with one another in the community. Glasser et al. write,

> It was only when Yahweh confronted them at Sinai and proclaimed the essence of their covenantal relation to him that they [Israel] began to sense themselves as a redeemed people, chosen by him to be his possession forever. The Book of the Covenant (Exod. 20–23) defined the boundaries of their existence as Yahweh's people.[20]

Salvation is never real as a communal experience until it is personalized as an individual experience. Whereas Israel may have spoken with one voice at Sinai, promising to do all that Yahweh had commanded, it was essential that the voice of every Israelite be heard in that pronouncement. This is why the sin of Achan was sufficient to attract God's wrath on all of Israel (Josh 7).

God's Covenant with the New Israel

On the day of Pentecost when the Holy Spirit came upon the believers in Christ, the Bible says that those believers boldly declared the saving grace of Christ. When Peter finished that inaugural message of the church, "Those who accepted his message were baptized and about three thousand were added to their number that day" (Acts 2:41). Among this multitude of converts were people from Parthia, Media, Mesopotamia, Judea, Cappadocia, Pontus, Asia, Phrygia, Pamphylia, Egypt, Libya, Cyrene, Crete, and Arabia. The Bible clearly identified these converts as "Jews and converts to Judaism" (Acts 2:5–12). On its first day, the church was not an ethnic church, rather it was a multicultural church.

Writing about the significance of Pentecost in the making of God's people, Glasser et al. state,

> With the event of the Holy Spirit on the day of Pentecost, God's redemptive activity shifted from working through a particular people (the descendants of Abraham via Isaac and Jacob and Israel) to working in the midst of all peoples. On that day the

19. Ibid., 145.
20. Glasser et al., *Announcing the Kingdom*, 83.

Multiculturalism

New Testament expression of the people of God, the church, was formed and empowered for its worldwide mission.[21]

In his invitation, Peter called the believers to remove themselves from this corrupt generation (Acts 2:40). They needed to separate themselves from the world so as to enter into a new covenant relationship with God. This is similar to the call Abraham received many generations past, to remove himself from his family, his ethnic group, his country, and go to a land Yahweh would show him. God's people are called to disconnect from ethnic, social, and political affiliations and enter into a new covenant relationship defined by the "I-Thou" relationship with God. Membership in this new covenant community, the church, would not be by family, ethnic, or any other form of group identity, but by a personal response to Jesus Christ in faith. The growth came as an incremental and not an exponential peoples movement as those individuals who believed were baptized, and "the Lord added to their number daily those who were being saved" (Acts 2:47).

In his general epistle to the church, Peter highlights once again the multicultural nature of this church. He addressed his first epistle to the elect, whom he also called "strangers in the world, scattered throughout Pontus, Galatia, Cappadocia, Asia and Bithynia, who have been chosen according to the foreknowledge of God the Father" (1 Pet 1:1–2). Though called out of the world, we have been called "into an inheritance that can never perish, spoil or fade" (1 Pet 1:4). We are the people of a new covenant. Peter described the church thus:

> a chosen people, a royal priesthood, a holy nation, a people belonging to God, that you may declare the praises of him who called you out of darkness into his wonderful light. Once you were not a people, but now you are the people of God; once you had not received mercy, but now you have received mercy. (1 Pet 2:9–10)

The same process by which Abraham was brought into a covenant relation with God—election—has now brought us into a covenant relationship with God. The same grace that elected Abraham and not his brothers has included us in the plan of God, though we were outside the covenant with Israel (Eph 2). The circumstances by which we Gentiles were brought into this covenant relationship is humbling enough to shut up the mouth of every arrogant and self-deluded believer who thinks by shear ethnicity, geography, or skin color he or she has a better access to the throne of grace

---

21. Ibid., 259.

Biblical Foundations for Multiculturalism

than other members of the body. We are simply "those who through the righteousness of our God and Savior Jesus Christ have received a faith as precious as ours" (2 Pet 1:1). It is by grace we have been saved. Let's affirm one another rather than consider ourselves more highly than others. Glasser and colleagues write that the fundamental characteristic of this new Christ-confessing community was that all its members received the gift of the Spirit. Acts 2:17–18 speaks of the Holy Spirit being poured out on "all people," male and female, young and old, slave and free. The very inclusiveness of this baptism constituted the democratization of the prophetic consciousness. All were empowered to bear witness to the resurrection (Acts 2:32).

At the foot of the cross the ground is level. There is "neither Jew nor Gentile, neither slave nor free," (Gal 3:28) but we all are seen as one body, one church, one Lord (Eph 4:4–5). Let's put aside the weights of sin that so easily pull us down and look unto Jesus who has called us into this privileged position of a covenant relationship with him. Let's strive to please him and not the earthly structures and social affiliations that will come to naught.

> *God's people must look beyond Babel with its narrow-minded greed and self-centeredness, its dwindling ziggurats and earthly pride cursed by God, and look towards a kingdom that emerges.*

In the New Testament church a new Israel was born. A new elect people was created. God entered into a new covenant with the remnant over which the Prince of Peace would reign. A new era has dawned on human history. God's people must look beyond Babel with its narrow-minded greed and self-centeredness, its dwindling ziggurats and earthly pride cursed by God, and look towards a kingdom that emerges, as the prophet said:

> The wolf will live with the lamb, the leopard will lie down with the goat, the calf and the lion and the yearling together; and a little child will lead them. The cow will feed with the bear, their young will lie down together, and the lion will eat straw like the ox. The infant will play near the cobra's den, the young child will put its hand into the viper's nest. They will neither harm nor destroy on all my holy mountain, for the earth will be filled with the knowledge of the Lord as the waters cover the sea. (Isa 11:6–9)

CREATED FOR MISSIO DEI (THE MISSION OF GOD)

Old Testament theologians have wrestled over the years to explain God's purpose in making mankind. No potter forms a vessel without a purpose. The unanimous consensus among theologians about God's purpose in creating mankind seems to be fellowship with God. In the creative act, God breathed into mankind a unique life source different from that of other living beings.

The story of creation and life in the garden depicts a close and personal relationship between God and humans, in which God delighted in the fellowship they shared. Beyond that fellowship, God gave mankind some clear and specific mandates in relation to nature and the rest of creation. These mandates bring into focus God's mission and the place of mankind in that mission.

The Idea of God's Mission in the Garden of Eden

Humanity's mission in the garden was clear and specific: "Be fruitful and increase in number; fill the earth and subdue it. Rule over the fish of the sea and the birds of the air and over every living creature that moves on the ground" (Gen 1:28). In the garden, God the master builder and creator invited mankind to partner with him in his creative work. We became his emissaries, his representatives, to rule over his creation and to conserve them with a sense of stewardship. Mankind was to multiply itself so as to extend the rule of God to the ends of the earth. This mandate best demonstrates what the writer of Genesis was attempting to convey when stating that "God created mankind in his own image" (Gen 1:27) Lasor, Hubbard, and Bush write, "The resemblance is dynamic, in that the human beings (Adam) in their personal relationships with other creatures become God's representative, with the natural right to explore, subdue, and use everything around them."[22]

From here on, wherever people would go on earth, they would make known the rule of God among the creatures of God. That was our mission. We manifest our true humanity when in words and deeds we truly represent our creator and advance his work on earth. Any work or word that removes focus from God and centers it on mankind is a distortion of the

---

22. Lasor, Hubbard, and Bush, *Old Testament Survey*, 78.

Biblical Foundations for Multiculturalism

plan and purpose of God for human beings. It is sinful to distort or misuse God's image in us.

Noah's Mission and Discipleship

Having previously established how as a result of sin mankind fell out of favor with God and then that God regretted having made them, in Noah God attempted to reclaim his mission. Noah was a fair representation of God's image. He was described as "a righteous man, blameless among the people of his time, and he walked with God" (Gen 6:9–10). These characteristics show that he was living out the true image of God in his personal life. God found in him a ray of hope for the preservation of mankind and a future perpetuation of his mission, so he involved Noah in his next plan for humanity. God intimated to Noah what he was about to do to the earth, which had gone utterly corrupt. Herein is the spirit of prophecy, for prophecy is God revealing his will to holy people who are in tune with him, so he can take them along in his plan for the world.

Beyond the cultural mandate of the garden, which called for husbandry of the created order, God assigns to Noah a new task in his larger plan of recreating the universe. Noah was to make (create) an ark with specific dimensions given by God himself. He was to take in a pair of all beasts of the field and birds of the air and keep custody of them along with the members of his family and anyone else who would heed his voice to flee from the wrath to come. God was going to clean the earth of its corruption, and through Noah and his companions bring into being a new order of existence.

Noah found himself at the heart of God's mission, creating an escape boat, preserving the creatures, and pleading with fallen mankind to repent. The dual mission of God that Glasser et al. call the cultural mandate and the divine mandate are both fulfilled in Noah's testimony of righteousness and his obedience in building the ark and preserving the creatures of God. Twice the Bible states, "Noah did everything just as God commanded him" (Gen 6:22; 7:5). The universality of the covenant that God made with Noah indicates that Noah was simply a partner with God in the implementation of his divine plan and purpose, rather than an exclusive beneficiary of God's grace. His mission and discipleship was God-centered, so he became a co-laborer with God in his act of remaking the world. Noah points us to

Multiculturalism

a universal rather than exclusive (particular) divine mission in which we have been invited to partake.

Abraham's Mission and Discipleship

In his call and election God made clear to Abraham his mission and his place within God's plan. The Lord outlined his promises to Abraham: "I will make you into a great nation and I will bless you; I will make your name great, and you will be a blessing. I will bless those who bless you and whoever curses you I will curse; and all peoples on earth will be blessed through you" (Gen 12:2–3). Whereas God was initiating a particular history of now dealing with individuals who would respond in faith to him and his plan and purpose, it is important to note that the ultimate goal was a universal redemption. God would bless Abraham exceedingly so he could become a blessing to others. God would bless those who blessed him and curse those who cursed him because God planned that through Abraham all the nations of the earth would be blessed.

The implication, therefore, contrary to what we had supposed earlier, is that the election of Abraham was not necessarily the rejection of other nations. The covenant with Abraham did not exclude the nations from the plan of God; rather, Abraham would be the bridge, the connection, through which the nations would be included in the covenant with God. Abraham's mission was to bear the name of the Lord among the nations. His call was to be a disciple to the nations around him, becoming the voice of God among them. In his encounters with Pharaoh and Abimelech, Abraham did not do quite a good job at being an evangelist to the nations, but in his intercession on behalf of Sodom and Gomorrah, he fulfilled very well this role of a missionary to the nations.

One must concede, however, that Abraham's faith and understanding of his mission unfolded with time. As he came to know the Lord he began to both trust him and depend on him. This appears in his dealing with Lot, who was willing to choose a place of abode before Abraham, his uncle. Abraham had brought him along the journey, and when strife ensued Abraham pleaded with him that they part peacefully. The older should have had the right of first choice, but Lot looked greedily at the lush, green plains of Sodom and quickly made his pick. Abraham, who had come to know that God was his provider, trusted enough to not think Lot's choice or decision could in any way impede God's plans for his life. This same faith in God's providence led him to that remarkable declaration before the king of Sodom, "With raised hand I have sworn an oath to the Lord, God Most High, Creator of heaven and earth, that I will accept nothing belonging to you, not even a thread or the strap of a sandal, so that you will never be able to say, 'I made Abram rich'" (Gen 14:22–23).

In the words of Lasor, Hubbard, and Bush, "God has freely chosen one man and his descendants through whom 'all the families of the earth shall find blessing,'" promising him land and nationhood.[23] The land and nation, however, remained a distant reality to both Abraham and his descendants through many generations. The land and nationhood were not to become the end of the story; they were supposed to be means to an end: the making of God's people, the ultimate mission of God.

Israel's Mission and Discipleship

A fundamental flaw in Israel's relationship with God from the time they settled in the land of Canaan till today is a deliberate refusal to embrace the fact that their mission in the world was to be a source of blessing to the nations. God said to Abraham, "in you all the families of the earth shall be blessed" (Gen 12:3 kjv). Israel's mission on earth was to be God's agent through whom the nations of the earth are brought into a covenant relationship with God. This mission presupposes an election. God elected Israel to himself among all the nations of the earth. On Mount Sinai, God said to Israel, "if you obey me fully and keep my covenant, then out of all nations you will be my treasured possession" (Exod 19:5). Somewhere along the way Israel saw this election as reflecting a special inherent character or quality that has distinguished them from the other nations and placed them morally and spiritually above them, and so instead of responding to the nations with an evangelistic or redemptive outlook, they withdrew from the nations and isolated themselves in fear of contamination and corruption. Israel saw the covenant relationship with God as an exclusive right and would not open the door of that relationship to other nations. This was probably the earliest example of "manifest destiny" at work in the world. Sadly though, it was for the sake of the nations that God had elected Israel. He spoke to them through his prophet Isaiah thus:

---

23. Ibid., 116.

Multiculturalism

> I, the Lord, have called you in righteousness; I will take hold of your hand. I will keep you and will make you to be a covenant for the people and a light for the Gentiles, to open eyes that are blind, to free captives from prison and to release from the dungeon those who sit in darkness. (Isa 42:6–7)

How much more direct could God have been in communicating to Israel her purpose in the world? Israel lost a grasp of this mandate because she held too tightly to a nationalistic identity and purpose. Israel saw her purpose in the world differently from how God saw it. She thought she was called for herself and for her own sake. Israel owed nothing to the rest of humanity and cared less what happened to them. She narrowly interpreted the pronouncement, "I will bless those who bless you, and whoever curses you I will curse" (Gen 12:3). She felt that the nations needed them, but they did not need the nations. Israel was God's chosen people and the rest of the world could go to hell. This narrow and prejudiced interpretation of her purpose in the world remains the reason why most Israelites have yet to accept Christ as the fulfillment of their hope. Let's pray that the church in America does not adopt this perspective for her mission.

The Mission of the Church

The church, the New Israel, is similar to the Old Israel in many ways. Born on the Day of Pentecost, the infant church ushered in a new dispensation in the plan of God for the world. The Bible records that on that Pentecost day, the disciples were together in one place when,

> Suddenly a sound like the blowing of a violent wind came from heaven and filled the whole house where they were sitting. They saw what seemed to be tongues of fire that separated and came to rest on each of them. All of them were filled with the Holy Spirit and began to speak in other tongues as the Spirit enabled them. (Acts 2:1–4)

That event was both unprecedented and never repeated in the same form ever since. It was a decisive moment when God acted in human history

Biblical Foundations for Multiculturalism

to usher in a new dispensation of his kingdom. A close look at that day's events reveals the momentous nature of this occurrence.

In concert with the wind and the tongues of fire, the speaking in tongues was part of a package of phenomenal events that ushered in the new era of God's work among people—that ushered in the birth of the church.[24] Whereas it brought believers to a higher experience of spirituality, it brought unbelievers to their knees and they yielded their lives to Christ in large numbers. The speaking in tongues reveals the message that the God of Israel is also God of the nations.[25] Macchia explains that at Babel humanity knew unity only in homogeneity of language and culture, but at Pentecost God's people experience unity in diversity of cultures and languages. At Babel, the people of the earth came together to build a tower that reached the heavens, but at Pentecost the people of God scattered to build the kingdom of God on earth. At Babel humanity sought pride and fulfillment in the works of its own hands, but at Pentecost humanity found fulfillment in the work of God. Through tongues, humanity, who were scattered at Babel were brought together in Jerusalem. Whereas at Babel one spoken language became confusing tongues that divided, at Pentecost a diversity of tongues became a unifying force. Whereas at Babel it looked as though the will of God had been disrupted as humanity was scattered due to confusing tongues, at Pentecost God's will for humanity was recaptured as diversity of tongues led to the scattering of God's people to take the good news to the ends of the earth.[26]

> *At Babel, the people of the earth came together to build a tower that reached the heavens, but at Pentecost the people of God scattered to build the kingdom of God on earth.*

The fact that the gospel of Christ was not ethnic or national good news but global good news became clear to the first-century church. Peter, after God had dealt with him on the issue of his ethnocentrism, declared to Cornelius and those gathered in his house, "God does not show favoritism but accepts from every nation the one who fears him and does what is right" (Acts 10:35). Paul nudged the inclusion of the Gentiles beyond Peter's universality of the gospel, taking it a step further. He boldly declared that he was called as a teacher and missionary to the Gentiles (1 Tim 2:7).

24. Unger, *New Testament Teaching on Tongues*, 27–34.
25. Glasser et al., *Announcing the Kingdom*, 52.
26. Macchia, "Babel and the Tongues of Pentecost," 35.

Multiculturalism

The Gentiles are part and parcel of the plan of God for the world. They have a central place in God's purpose, and the church must focus on a mission to the world, not just an ethnic group.

The twenty-first century American church, however, seems to have lost touch with the global nature of this gospel. The idea of manifest destiny is once again limiting the ability of God's people to fulfill God's mission for them and actualize their purpose in the world. The current rise of neo-fundamentalism and the emergence of the Tea Party movement raise a call for a return to the "Good Old Days" of America. God's plan and purpose for mankind is once again seen through the lens of manifest destiny. A clarion call sounds for a return to the principles established by the founding fathers. Diversity is seen by some who share these ideologies as un-American and deviant. Sadly, these individuals may have refused to engage the truth of the very principles established by their founding fathers. American manifest destiny flaunts the idea that America was "destined to expand democratic institutions in North America, which gave the nation a superior moral right to govern areas where other interests would not respect this goal."[27] John L. O'Sullivan, who was thought to have originated this idea, wrote concerning this nation in 1839:

> Yes, we are the nation of progress, of individual freedom, of universal enfranchisement. Equality of rights is the cynosure of our union of States, the grand exemplar of the correlative equality of individuals; and while truth sheds its effulgence, we cannot retrograde, without dissolving the one and subverting the other. We must onward to the fulfillment of our mission—to the entire development of the principle of our organization—freedom of conscience, freedom of person, freedom of trade and business pursuits, universality of freedom and equality. This is our high destiny, and in nature's eternal, inevitable decree of cause and effect we must accomplish it. All this will be our future history, to establish on earth the moral dignity and salvation of man—the immutable truth and beneficence of God. For this blessed mission to the nations of the world, which are shut out from the life-giving light of truth, has America been chosen; and her high example shall smite unto death the tyranny of kings, hierarchs, and oligarchs, and carry the glad tidings of peace and good will where myriads now endure an existence scarcely more enviable than that of beasts

---

27. "John L. O'Sullivan on Manifest Destiny, 1839."

Biblical Foundations for Multiculturalism

of the field. Who, then, can doubt that our country is destined to be *the great nation* of futurity?[28]

O'Sullivan, like Old Testament prophets, saw America's purpose not as a self-serving purpose, but as a "mission to the nations of the world." How exciting! America's purpose could not end with acquisition of Indian lands, annexation of Mexico, and the establishment of a self-serving government. It must be seen as a stewardship. God has placed this nation here at such a time as this to be light to the darkness of this world and salt to the corruption and decay of the human generation.

Leading up to this point, Israel has been painted as a nation that turned from God, or more specifically, thought itself higher than other nations and in so doing kept its message to itself. The American church must be careful that we do not castrate the gospel of Jesus because we are holding ethnic and racial identities and preferences in greater honor than the mission of God for this great nation. A house built on a hill cannot be hidden, and people do not light a candle and put it under the table, but set it in a place where it can shine light to the whole room (cf. Matt 5:13–16).

KOINONIA—THE CONCEPT OF GOD'S PEOPLE

According to Glasser et al., the purpose of the church derives from its mission to the world, which is preaching the gospel to the world as a witness for Christ. He points out that at Pentecost God began the work of reversing the scattering and hostility of nations that began at Babel. God was on a unifying mission.[29] Moreover, the identity of the church at Pentecost was not shaped by ethnicity, language, or cultural identity but rather by "their spiritual oneness" in which they devoted themselves to the apostles' teachings, to fellowship, and to communal prayer. The result was *koinonia*—fellowship or oneness.

The Greek word *koinonia* means "fellowship." This fellowship is not mere association with another person; it embodies the ideas of association and participation whereby the individual shares a common experience with others in community.[30] Panikulam examines Paul's use of the word *koinonia* to signify a present and future reality. In Pauline theology, *koi-*

---

28. Ibid.
29. Glasser et al., *Announcing the Kingdom*, 264.
30. Cf. Panikulam, *Koinonia in the New Testament*, 1.

Multiculturalism

nonia as the experience of God's people in community is a present reality within the present community of God's people, but it extends beyond that through our spiritual fellowship which finds its consummation at the second coming (*parousia*). He points out two significant concepts of *koinonia* in Pauline theology:

1. Christ-centric life: Life lived for Christ
2. Communitarian life: Life lived in community[31]

The Pauline idea of fellowship with Christ is seen as salvation for the individual as well as that individual's fellowship with others in Christ.[32]

Salvation, which is an intrinsic prerequisite to this fellowship, involves *klesis*, a "calling." Just as Abram was called out of Ur of the Chaldeans to a land the Lord would give him, the believer is "called out" from a religious, cultural, and social identity that had previously defined him, into a new identity. Those who are called by God become his own possession. They are removed from a history that pointed toward eternal death to a history that now points toward eternal life. *Klesis* means we have been called out from an old identity into a new identity rooted in personal salvation rather than a cultural experience. We have been called out from an old community—our ethnic, cultural, social, and political communities. We are called into a new community called the church. If this logic holds, it means that the new identity and community are not defined by our previous associations. Our previous identities have become obsolete. Paul put it very succinctly: "Therefore, if anyone is in Christ, he is a new creation, the old has gone, the new has come" (2 Cor 5:17).

The bond of fellowship that joins believers in Christ is stronger than the bonds that have united us with our nonbelieving biological and ethnic family and friends. Through the blood of Christ, we enter into an eternal fellowship that far supersedes any human ties.

THE CONCEPT OF GOD'S KINGDOM

Christian thought includes the belief that the church is the visible representation of the kingdom of God on earth. The church is seen as the "ecclesiastical kingdom."[33] This idea of the church as the ecclesiastical kingdom is

---

31. Ibid.
32. Snyder, *Models of the Kingdom*, 67.
33. Ibid., 72.

Biblical Foundations for Multiculturalism

prominent when we are called a "chosen generation . . . royal priesthood . . . a holy nation" (1 Pet 2:4–9). Whereas Peter, in 1 Peter 1:1–2, identifies the members of this church as diverse and scattered all over Asia, Bithynia, and the environs, he nevertheless now refers to them as a unit. He calls them one generation, one line of priests, one nation. He has no problem affirming this unity since he had already established that our unity derives from a common election by the foreknowledge of God, through the sanctifying work of the Spirit and the cleansing by the blood of Christ (1 Pet 1:2). This unity is neither ethnic nor racial; rather, it is both spiritual and experiential. All who by faith have been elected, cleansed, and sanctified by the blood of the lamb become *bona fide* members of the body of Christ.

The ecclesiastical kingdom model of the church has received one-sided attention from Christians since the church—whether in its Episcopal or papal structures or in American congregational forms—has often seen itself as the harbinger of the kingdom. Membership in the earthly church structures has often been seen as synonymous to membership in the kingdom. This view is held even when the church structures are corrupt and ungodly. Snyder argues, "the kingdom of God is a reality and set of values to be lived out now, in the present order, in radical obedience to the gospel and in opposition to the powers of the present age."[34] He calls this perspective of the kingdom a counter-system model. To this counter-system model he assigns certain distinguishing characteristics:

1. *Prophetic* in character: It calls for justice in society in accordance with the values of the kingdom.

2. *Christocentric* ethics: Christ is the example for a kingdom lifestyle. The kingdom is seen as "Christianized culture."

3. *Peaceable* kingdom: This kingdom motif calls for a renunciation of violence and retaliation and suggests a total surrender to God to judge the wicked and to right injustices.[35]

If we believe Jesus to be the messiah, we must see the church as the remnant of Israel. If he is the Son of man, we must be the saints of his glorious reign. If he is the new Moses, we must be the new Israel. According to John Bright,

> For the true Israel—the people of the kingdom—are not those who are Israelites by race, nor yet those who are of that elite group in Israel who know and keep the external law, but those individual

---

34. Ibid., 77.
35. Ibid., 77–78.

men (and women), however lowly and weak, who have in their heart and deed signified their obedience to the calling of God.[36]

The kingdom motif acknowledges the sovereignty of God by seeking shalom and justice for the poor and oppressed. In this kingdom motif God takes the side of the poor and oppressed, standing in opposition to the principalities and powers, both visible and invisible. This view of the kingdom sees the church in a special light. It sees the church as "an actual social community, a new social reality, a people who in fact share life together day by day."[37] The church's communion is not merely spiritual or eschatological. It is a shared life in space and time, a way of living out the gospel together in the midst of the present society and history. The church is the messianic community that now visibly embodies the prophetic reality of the kingdom.

Snyder unapologetically links liberation theology to Marxists ideology and subsequently anchors that linkage on a kingdom motif. According to him, Marxism should probably be best understood as a "secularized materialistic" version of the Christian idea of the kingdom of God. Liberation theology, he argues, desires to see society transformed now into the kingdom of God. It seeks a new society of justice and equality. Contrary to Marxism, whose utopia is the product of human action, this kingdom ideal becomes reality as a result of God's action among his people.[38]

CHAPTER SUMMARY

This chapter focused on biblical foundations for multiculturalism. The conversation began with the idea of our creation in the image of God (*imago Dei*). It progressed into a discussion of the idea of covenant in God's dealing with humans. This covenant idea started with Noah and runs through Abraham, the Old Israel, and to the church, called the New Israel. We discussed the mission of God and the kingdom of God within the context of these covenant relationships.

We concluded that the image of God that we reflect is neither biological nor physical but spiritual. We concluded also that God's mission is not an ethnocentric mission, neither is it based on any racial or ethnic

---

36. Bright, *The Kingdom of God*, 219–20.
37. Snyder, *Models of the Kingdom*, 77–84.
38. Ibid., 116–17.

prerogatives or preferences. On the contrary, it is a cosmic mission that targets all humanity regardless of ethnicity, race, and geography. We concluded with a discussion of the idea of God's people sharing a spiritual identification based on a faith relationship with God through Jesus Christ. These compelling arguments on the biblical basis for multiculturalism undergird the differences between multiculturalism, Marxism, and social justice as found in multiculturalism.

7

Shalom: A New Paradigm for Multiculturalism

THIS CHAPTER ENGAGES THE shalom motif within the multicultural context. It defines the shalom context and provides an introduction to shalom community that identifies its characteristics.

SHALOM AND MULTICULTURALISM

From the Bible we can derive unique lessons about multiculturalism. Both the concrete objects of life and society and the nonconcrete ones like culture are equally God's creation. He created humans in his image and appointed them partners with him in his creative work by becoming the originators and agents of culture as we know it today. Hence, multicultural education becomes an essential vehicle for developing and conserving this created order.[1] Understanding multiculturalism based on biblical principles gives us a totally different perspective on how we should see and relate to others. Let's compare two approaches to multiculturalism: the contemporary secular perspective and an assumed biblical perspective. Table 7.1 summarizes the comparison.

---

1. Wolters, *Creation Regained*.

Table 7.1: Two Approaches to Multiculturalism

	Contemporary Secular Perspective of Multiculturalism	Assumed Biblical Perspective of Multiculturalism
Perspectives on culture	Cultural relativism: All cultures are equal and there is no ideal, standard culture.	Christ's universal authority is above all cultures: There are absolute truths that apply to all people in all cultures.
Rationale for Multiculturalism	Social and political inequality stem from long histories of oppression to minority cultures and ethnic groups.	Human sin, alienation from God, and God's commandment to love the Lord and one's neighbor make openness to multiculturalism imperative.
Goal of multicultural education	Humanization and building educational systems and society characterized by equity, fairness, and social justice	Fulfillment of God's command to overcome alienation, estrangement, and hostility between God the creator and human beings and between humans beings and their fellow humans
Implementation of multicultural education	Changing curriculum by integrating minority cultural values, content, and pedagogies and advocating for social justice	Practicing and applying the great commandment in our daily lives and walk

The teachings of Jesus and other biblical foundations present us with a new framework for multiculturalism, called the shalom model, by which a Christian appropriation of the principles of multiculturalism can lead to a community characterized by shalom.

A Shalom Model

To understand the shalom model, we must first understand what the word *shalom* means. The word *shalom*, a Hebrew word (שָׁלוֹם), is generally translated to mean "peace" or "wholeness." Yoder claims that Scripture uses this word with three different meanings that point to peace and wholeness: a material and physical state of being, relationships, and a moral sense of duty.[2] Expanding on these three ideas, he suggests that as a material and physical state, shalom seeks harmony for people's physical and material well-being. In Genesis 37:14, Jacob asked his son Joseph to go to his brothers and check on their *shalom* (or well-being). This points to health and physical well-being, including the fact that their material needs were being met. So a state of shalom ensures good health and absence of war and deprivations. The second idea of shalom as relationships speaks to personal harmony, harmony with people around one, and harmony with God. This kind of harmony is impossible in an environment devoid of social justice and equity. The last meaning suggests that shalom is the presence of moral and ethical relationships characterized by honesty, integrity, and straightforward character. It is the absence of deceit, lies, and hypocrisy.[3]

In his book of essays *Educating for Shalom: Essays on Christian Higher Education*, Nicholas Wolterstorff "rejects the maturation, socialization, and humanization models of education, calling instead to teach for justice and shalom."[4] In the introduction to this book, Clarence Jodersma writes concerning Wolterstorff's idea of shalom:

> shalom is more than a vision for Wolterstorff; it is a command to humans living here and now, in fallen world, in a society that is filled with pain, suffering, and woundedness.... Shalom as a command asks us to respond—now—to the cries and tears of human suffering: to pangs of the hungry, to those abandoned to refugee camps for generations, to squalor of inner cities, to the places of war around the globe.[5]

According to Wolterstorff's idea of shalom, we cannot remain indifferent to the plight of those around us but must address the call to justice and action here and now.

The Community of Shalom

> The wolf will live with the lamb, the leopard will lie down with the goat, the calf and the lion and the yearling together; and a

---

2. Yoder, *Shalom*.
3. Cf. Ps 34:14; 37; Yoder, *Shalom*.
4. Wolterstorff, *Educating for Shalom*, vii.
5. Ibid., xiii.

Shalom: A New Paradigm for Multiculturalism

little child will lead them. The cow will feed with the bear, their young will lie down together, and the lion will eat straw like the ox. The infant will play near the cobra's den, and the young child will put its hand into the viper's nest. They will neither harm nor destroy on all my holy mountain, for the earth will be filled with the knowledge of the Lord as the waters cover the sea. (Isa 11:6–9)

The prophet Isaiah paints a picture of this community of shalom for God's people Israel. We hope the idea of this community is not just a far-fetched dream for God's people, but can be a present reality and a future hope that we all strive for. This goal can be accomplished in two stages. First, all Christians must come to accept that every human being is created in the image of God (*imago Dei*) and every human being needs to be treated honorably and respectfully. The idea of the image of God can be extended and supported through four principles regarding human interactions:

1. Cultural identity
2. Cross-cultural competence
3. Contextualized pedagogy
4. Social justice

Through these four principles, the eventual goal of multicultural education can be accomplished. Figure 7.1 presents this model.

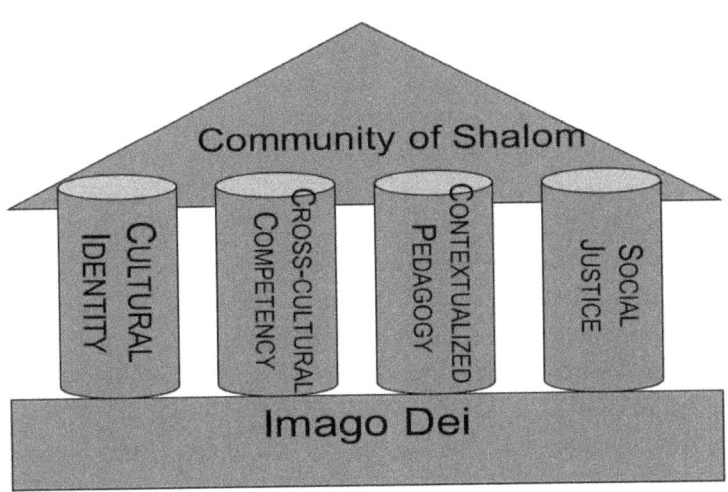

Figure 7.1: The Shalom Community Model

Multiculturalism

Cultural Identity. A fact that Christians must live with is that our faith is neither received nor practiced in a cultural vacuum. People come to Christ within cultural situations and cross-cultural contexts. Both the bearer of the message and the recipient are products of their own cultural experiences. Quite often diverse cultural and linguistic elements mediate the gospel that has been received as the message of salvation. This gospel is usually packaged in cultural frames of reference and conveyed through language. However, awareness and affirmation of our diverse cultural identities acknowledges the fact that cultural homogeneity is not a prerequisite for admission into the plan of God for salvation. At Pentecost the Holy Spirit suspended cultural and linguistic barriers and made the good news accessible to everyone present.

It must also be clear to all Christians that proclaiming the good news does not need to impose the missionary's culture and worldview on the believer in order for that believer to be truly assimilated into the family of God. Only in terms of faith and belief is God's kingdom homogenous, otherwise it is essentially a culturally diverse kingdom (cf. Rev 7:9–10).

Cross-cultural Competence. Regarding this principle, we must first present an understandable concept of cultural competence. Cultural competence has been defined as "a set of congruent behaviors, attitudes, and policies that come together in a system, agency, or among professionals that enables effective work in cross-cultural situations."[6] According to these authors, *culture* refers to integrated patterns of human behavior that include the language, thoughts, communications, actions, customs, beliefs, values, and institutions of racial, ethnic, religious, or social groups. *Competence* implies having the capacity to function effectively as an individual and an organization within the context of the cultural beliefs, behaviors, and needs presented by consumers and their communities. Thus, the idea of cultural competence refers to the ability to understand and function effectively within a social setting with the necessary tools for dealing with diverse social and cultural issues and perspectives.

This interpretation of cultural competence suggests that the ability to understand the complexities of cultures and worldviews represented in a multicultural society is essential to effective professional practices and interpersonal relationships. The absence of cultural competence in a culturally diverse society should be seen as a disability or a disadvantage. Cultural incompetence leads to insensitivity, disrespect, and disharmony. These are

---

6. Cross, Bazron, Dennis, and Isaac, *Toward a Culturally Competent System.*

not virtues; they are vices. Unfortunately, some people see their inability to understand and get along with people who are culturally different from them as positive. That is not so. To be culturally competent is to be aware and sensitive to the differences in values, beliefs, and personal concerns of others.[7]

Whereas cultural competence speaks to the need to understand and effectively function with awareness of and respect of the complex cultural variables in one's society, cross-cultural competence refers to the ability to function effectively when moving away from one's community to another country or culture that is different. Cross-cultural competences speak to one's comfort level in traversing cultural boundaries and being able to function effectively in that new context. The paramount Christian mandate is recorded in Matthew 28:19–20, "Therefore go and make disciples of all nations, baptizing them in the name of the Father and of the Son and of the Holy Spirit." We call this the Great Commission, not the Great Suggestion. A commission is a charge, an order. This order comes from the Chief Commander of our army, Jesus Christ himself. To be his disciples across the nations requires more than cultural competency, it requires cross-cultural competency. It is only logical that in a global age, God's people see themselves as global citizens so they can effectively work to make the kingdoms of this world the kingdom of our God and his Christ. Cross-cultural competency is impossible without an explicit endorsement of the validity of other cultures.

Contextualized Pedagogy. Should we dare to challenge the retreat of God's people from public educational settings to private parochial and home schools? Yes, the public school systems have become spiritual battlefields where the souls of our children stand in danger of exploitation by secular humanistic interests and philosophies. What section of our society is not equally challenged? How many of our churches have become social clubs and make-you-feel-good support groups? The idea of contextualized pedagogies demands that our instructional strategies—whether in the public educational settings, the private parochial schools, or home schools—are sensitive to the needs of the learner and the educational goals. The goal of education is not just to impart knowledge of the languages, sciences, and mathematics to the younger generation, but to develop informed and responsible citizens who are able to function effectively in a democracy. Our educational institutions must operate in fidelity to these goals.

---

7. Norton, *Dual Perspectives.*

The shalom model comprises several features. First of all, the essential idea of a community of shalom comes from the Bible and the theme of the creation-fall-redemption process, which is articulated by Wolters. In addition, this model clearly identifies multiculturalism's role as the intervention that "participates in the ongoing creative work of God, to be God's helper in executing to the end the blueprint for his masterpiece."[8]

This model is comprehensive and covers theory and practices from the personal as well as the social/community levels of existence. It encompasses knowledge, skills, and dispositions for effective training in the field of multicultural education. This model also advocates an effective change strategy that starts from the individual level to the community by means of the four intervention principles.

CULTURE AS A CREATION OF GOD: CULTURAL IDENTITY

God created diversity and loves it. God's creation story began by celebrating all the varieties in the universe (Gen 1 and 2), "the morning stars sang together and all the angels shouted for joy" (Job 38:7). The Bible ends by showing a heavenly scene where all peoples, tribes, and languages come before his throne to worship him (Rev 7:9). When God created the universe, he definitely loved the universe with its diversity. When he had finished his work, he looked at its beauty and diversity and celebrated them (Gen 1:10, 18, 25, 31). Therefore, to celebrate creation is to celebrate diversity, including the diversity of people and their cultures.[9]

God created two realities: the physical world and nonphysical entities such as marriage (Gen 2:24), and government authority (Rom 13:1–2; 1 Pet 2:13). God appointed humans who have been created in his image and likeness to rule the nonphysical world through culture and social structures. Therefore, the redeemed human beings, as God's partners, need to embrace culture and develop a positive cultural identity in order to transform society for good, as God desires. Cultural diversity affirms God's creation.

Cultural identity refers to the cultural features characteristic of a particular group, together with one's feelings about those features and one's understanding of how they are (or are not) reflected in oneself.[10] Cultural

---

8. Wolters, *Creation Regained*, 38.
9. Elmer, *Cross-Cultural Conflict*.
10. Ferdman and Horenczyk, "Cultural Identity and Immigration," 86.

Shalom: A New Paradigm for Multiculturalism

identity consists of three components: the person's ethnic affiliation; the individual's feelings about the cultural features ascribed to the group; and the individual's view of where, how, and to what degree the group culture is reflected in the self.[11]

Kowalski categorized cultural identity in three ways: (1) human universals; (2) group associations; and (3) individual personality. Human universals are the features that all human beings share with all others, regardless of differences in culture, such as biological features, emotions, social constructs, and values. Group identity is divided into three categories: the unalterable (ethnicity, gender, age, and family/ancestry); the alterable (nationality, religion, economic status, social class); and the self-selected (profession, academic association, organizational membership, etc.). Individual personality ultimately shapes cultural identity. It is established based on an individual's unique thoughts and beliefs. Individuals decide to what extent each group association determines one's personal cultural identity. Figure 7.2 diagrams Kowalski's theory on cultural identity.[12]

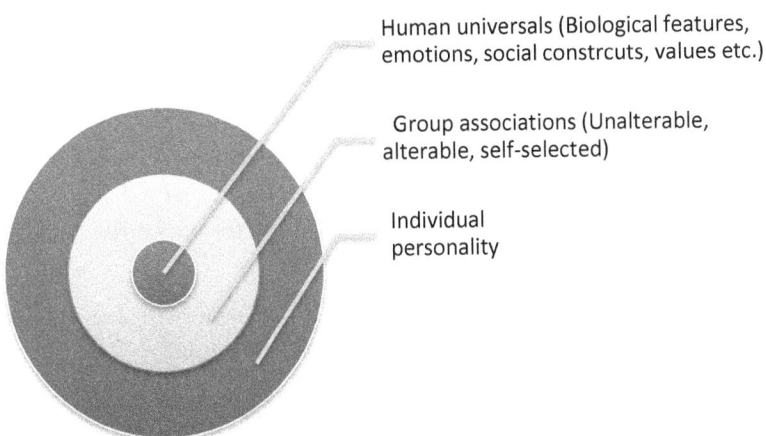

Figure 7.2: Kowalski's Theory on Cultural Identity

The cultural identity of an immigrant person living in a culturally diverse society undergoes a unique cultural-identity reshaping, affected by his or her acculturation process. Each cultural/racial group has a distinct cultural heritage, and an individual moves through different stages when forming a cultural identity.

11. Ferdman and Horenczyk, "Cultural Identity and Immigration."
12. Kowalski, "Three Dimensions of Cultural Identity," 256–63.

Multiculturalism

Cultural identity is a dynamic and complex feeling that consists of a sense of belonging to one or more ethnic groups. It defines the way an individual identifies or positions the self in a different cultural context. James Banks suggests that cultural identity is an evolving concept from focusing on self-acceptance to the acceptance and valuing of others. He identifies six stages in the development of cultural identity:

- Stage 1 (cultural psychology captivity): Individuals internalize the negative stereotypes and beliefs about their cultural groups that are institutionalized within the larger society and may exemplify cultural self-rejection and low self-esteem.

- Stage 2 (cultural encapsulation): Individuals within this stage often have newly discovered their cultural consciousness and try to limit their social engagement to their own cultural group.

- Stage 3 (cultural identity clarification): Individuals are able to clarify their personal attitudes and cultural identity and develop clarified positive attitudes toward their cultural group.

- Stage 4 (biculturalism): Individuals have a healthy sense of cultural identity and the psychological characteristics to participate successfully in their own cultural community as well as any other setting.

- Stage 5 (multiculturalism and reflective nationalism): Individuals possess clarified, reflective, and positive personal, cultural, and national identifications along with positive attitudes towards other racial, cultural, and ethnic groups.

- Stage 6 (globalism and global competency): Individuals have reflective and clarified national and global identifications.[13]

CROSS-CULTURAL COMPETENCE: A KINGDOM IMPERATIVE

As Micah 6:8 states in the Old Testament, God requires us to act justly, to love mercy, and to walk humbly with God. But questions still remain: how do we do that? In order to accomplish this, what cultural competences and skills do we need? We must understand that there are many different cultural values, traditions, and approaches that may make one uncomfortable. Hence, one of the multicultural education objectives is to help individuals

---

13. Banks, "Teaching for Social Justice, Diversity, and Citizenship," 295–97.

become culturally competent by equipping them with cross-cultural skills. All individuals need to accept their own ethnic and cultural identities first, then they need to be competent enough to relate with people from other ethnicities and cultures.[14]

> Cultural competence in education refers to the ability to successfully teach students who come from other cultures other than your own. It entails acquiring complex awareness and sensitivities, various bodies of knowledge, and a set of skills that, taken together, underlie effective cross-cultural teaching.[15]

What does a culturally competent person look like? Boutte focuses on how a personal perspective on culture changes over time when interacting with other cultures. The value and attitude of a culturally competent person is described in stage three of his framework on the stages of multicultural growth. According to him, a culturally competent person actively seeks learning opportunities from other cultures and ethnicities by appreciating and respecting them. This model illustrates how an individual can develop from holding a one-dimensional perspective to incorporating a multidimensional one. Table 7.2 provides more detail.[16]

Table 7.2: Stages of Multicultural Growth

	Stage 1	Stage 2	Stage 3
Level of self-awareness	My perspective is right (the only one).	My perspective is one of many.	My perspective is changing and being enhanced.
Emotional response to difference	Fear, rejection, denial We're all alike	Interest, awareness, openness	Appreciation, respect, joy, enthusiasm Active seeking
Mode of cultural interaction	Isolation, avoidance, hostility	Integration, interaction, acceptance	Transforming, internalizing, rewarding
Approach to teaching	Eurocentric and ethnocentric curriculum	Learning about other cultures	Learning from other cultures
Approach to management	Mono-cultural, autocratic, directive	Compliance, tolerance	Collaborative, valuing diversity, maximizing potential

14. Banks, *Teaching Strategies for Ethnic Studies.*
15. Diller and Moule, *Cultural Competence,* 5.
16. Boutte, *Multicultural Education.*

Multiculturalism

The critical question is, how can we change from stage 1 or 2 to stage 3? What kinds of competencies and skills are needed to advance to stage 3? There are several models of cultural competence. Agyeman suggests five steps to cultural competence:

1. Valuing diversity by accepting and respecting differences

2. Having the ability to undertake cultural self-assessment in order to see how one's actions affect people from other cultures

3. Being aware of the dynamics that exist when cultures mix, such as the understandable mistrust of historically oppressed groups toward members of a dominant culture

4. Institutionalizing cultural and traditional knowledge that will enhance an organization's ability to serve diverse populations

5. Developing approaches to service delivery that show understanding of diversity between and within cultures[17]

Cross et al. identified five areas of multicultural competencies, including awareness and acceptance of differences, self-awareness, dynamics of difference, knowledge of students' culture, and adaptation of skills.[18] Atwater developed a model of cultural competence training that consists of two approaches: cultural knowledge training and color-consciousness training.[19] The former training emphasizes learning about cultural differences and cultural learning styles, while the color-consciousness training approach emphasizes a fundamental shift in teachers' conceptual thinking about racism, their own racial attitudes and identity, and the effects of skin color and institutional discrimination on the opportunities of nonwhite students. DomNwachukwu writes about cultural values adjustment as a way for individuals' cultural values and preferences to be challenged and revised for successful adaptation to new and more diverse cultural settings.[20]

Cross-cultural competence is a powerful tool with which we can build the peaceful community God has commanded. The Bible clearly indicates that cross-cultural competence would be an essential feature of God's kingdom as well as a prerequisite for mission among other cultures and

---

17. Agyeman, "Steps to Becoming Culturally Competent Communicators."
18. Cross et al., *Toward a Culturally Competent System.*
19. Atwater, "An Investigation of Teacher's Color-Blind Racial Attitudes."
20. DomNwachukwu, *Chinaka Samuel.*

ethnicities. Multicultural education can be seen as the attempt to transform the world by educating all individuals with full cross-cultural competencies.

Cross-cultural competency is an essential element of the kingdom motif. All people bear the image of God. The reason God chose Abraham and his descendants was to bless the whole world through them if they obey God's commandments. This promise of blessing all nations went through Abraham to his descendants until the coming of Jesus. In fact, Jesus was cross-culturally competent. He knew that embracing diversity was essential to the ministry of restoring God's plan for creation. He crossed the boundaries that traditional Jews had erected. He talked to a Samaritan woman whom Jewish leaders would have considered immoral. He associated with groups such as tax collectors and sinners (Luke 7:34). His disciples also put cross-cultural ministry as a top priority.

Paul clearly mentioned diversity in Ephesians 2:14, saying, "for he himself is our peace, who has made both one, and has broken down the middle wall of separation." He also proclaimed that we are all equal in Galatians 3:28: "There is neither Jew nor Gentile, neither slave nor free, nor is there male and female, for you are all one in Christ Jesus." The New Testament church embraced all peoples by uniting Jews and Gentiles. The early church believers were of one heart and mind (Acts 4:32).

CROSS-CULTURAL COMPETENCE: A MISSION IMPERATIVE

In Genesis 12:3, God said to Abraham "I will bless those who bless you, and whoever curses you I will curse, and all people on earth will be blessed through you." The same promise was continued to Isaac. In Genesis 26:4, God said, "through your offspring all nations on earth will be blessed." Likewise, God said to Jacob, "all people on earth will be blessed through you and your offspring" (Gen 28:14). However, God's promise was not fulfilled through the Israelites because of their disobedience. They did not live their lives as channels of blessing to all nations.

God is seeking to restore the relationship with all of humanity created in his image. Just as he searched for Adam in the garden, he is searching today for every human being across the world. Jesus commanded his followers to make disciples of all nations (the Greek word *ethnos* means "people"; Matt 28:16–20). He also challenged us to be cross-cultural witnesses beyond Judea and Samaria and to the very ends of the earth (Acts 1:7–8).

Multiculturalism

The biblical mandate for cross-cultural ministry is rooted in the very character of God. He calls Christians and gives them the task of fulfilling his purpose throughout the earth by making disciples of all nations and leading them to obey Christ. This challenge compels God's people to be missionaries by crossing cultural, social, economic, linguistic, ethnic, and personal barriers in order to accomplish his grand plan.

SOCIAL JUSTICE: A CHRISTOCENTRIC PARADIGM

> I hate, I despise your religious festivals; your assemblies are a stench to me. Even though you bring me burnt offerings and grain offerings, I will not accept them. Though you bring choice fellowship offerings, I will have no regard for them. Away with the noise of your songs! I will not listen to the music of your harps. But let justice roll on like a river, righteousness like a never-failing stream! (Amos 5:21–24)

Beginning from Genesis and ending in Revelation, the Bible resounds with the theme of social justice. It was out of a hunger for justice that Moses, while being raised as Pharaoh's son, struck and killed an Egyptian who was oppressing a Hebrew. It was because of God's commitment to justice and fair play that Ahab was condemned for killing Naboth and taking his rightful inheritance of his vineyard. All of the Old Testament prophets cried out for justice and fair play.

The passage quoted above from the prophet Amos very much speaks to our generation. Our age is full of individuals who are righteous bigots, religious racists, and prejudiced born-again Christians. We are a generation that has "created God in our own image." The same breath with which we sing his praise is the same breath with which we condemn his judgment when we speak ill of those in his creation who happen to be different from us. Amos told his generation that their religious activities were meaningless noise and useless oblations. When God's people fail to plead the cause of the oppressed and downtrodden, when we fail to speak for those without voices and seek release for the oppressed, our Christianity becomes a meaningless oblation.

What does social justice mean? Nieto and Bode define it "as a philosophy and approach and actions that embody treating all people with fairness, respect, dignity, and generosity."[21] To expand our understanding of social justice, Young argues that the issue of oppression should be addressed, identifying five faces of oppression:

1. Exploitation
2. Marginalization
3. Powerlessness
4. Cultural imperialism
5. Violence[22]

Social justice is taking sides with the weak and powerless. It is becoming a brother to the dispossessed. During his earthly ministry, as he entered Nazareth, Jesus Christ announced that his mission on earth was to "proclaim good news to the poor. He has sent me to proclaim freedom for the prisoners and recovery of sight for the blind, to set the oppressed free, to proclaim the year of the Lord's favor" (Luke 4:18–19). Many contemporary Christians are willing to donate their last penny to assist in taking the gospel to the unreached peoples of Asia, Africa, and South America, but when that unreached person is reached, converted, and brought into the United States as their next-door neighbor, they build an invisible wall between themselves and that individual because he/she is "different." Some of us are ready to fight for the rights of people who are being oppressed in Muslim countries, but are comfortable paying workers less than minimum wage in our companies, oppressing the aliens among us, and ensuring that they do not attain social mobility in our own society. Amos called Israelites of his time "cows of Bashan" who "oppress the poor and crush the needy" (Amos 4:1).

The Lord not only condemns injustice, he condemns those who see injustice and fail to confront it. So many Christians of our age are nonresponsive to injustice. We have become comfortable with avoidance. Someone called it "a conspiracy of silence." To such people the Bible says, "Woe to them that are at ease in Zion, and trust in the mountain of Samaria, which are named chief of the nations, to whom the house of Israel came!" (Amos 6:1 kjv). To fight for justice is to take sides with God in a cosmic battle. God has already declared his stand among the oppressed and down-trodden.

---

21. Nieto and Bode, *Affirming Diversity*, 11.
22. Young, "Five Faces of Oppression."

Multiculturalism

Believers in Christ must take a stand with their God if they are certain he is their God.

Much biblical evidence affirms that all people, nations, languages, and tribes are to be joined together as a family without racial or cultural separation or segregation. God created all human beings in his image and likeness. Therefore, all human beings possess an inherent dignity, meaning, and worth. All races, cultures, and ethnic groups have the same status and unique value that result from bearing the image of God. Therefore, the failure to reflect the image of God—as evidenced by ethnic, racial, and cultural segregation, division, and separation—is sin. Hence, multicultural education is an intentional process of not only advocating, but also implementing social justice in the educational setting. It is a change process towards the elimination of inequalities and unfairness in the education system and the larger society. If it is good for the educational setting, it is even better for the church.

Hernandez points out that multicultural education focuses on significant educational change, which occurs as we provide dynamic teaching, learning environments, and opportunities that reflect the ideals of equity and excellence.[23] This requires that students develop decision-making and social-action skills so they can take personal, social, and civic action to make their society and the world more democratic and humane. Sleeter and Grant criticize the theory-based interventions of multicultural education, which only promote adding diversity in a school or classroom.[24] They advocate multicultural education as facilitating social reconstruction and justice. Students should be aware of the injustices of society, reject them, and learn how to acquire constructive responses towards their elimination.

The idea of social action must be at the core of our engagement with multiculturalism. Gorski suggests three pathways of change for social action that focus on multicultural education: (1) the transformation of self, (2) the transformation of schools and schooling, and (3) the transformation of society[25]

Across these three contexts, multicultural education provides insight for the individual and for society that also transforms schools (and hopefully churches) into more participative and collaborative settings where all children (and all of God's people) can share, develop, and create learning (or

---

23. Hernandez, *Multicultural Education*.
24. Sleeter and Grant, *Making Choices for Multicultural Education*.
25. Gorski, *Multicultural Education and the Internet*.

worship) opportunities together. Multicultural education is an intentional intervention that removes educational and social inequality and unjust treatment. Removing these negatives opens the way for a state of shalom.

CHAPTER SUMMARY

Chapter 7 has engaged a new way of looking at multiculturalism, with the shalom motif. This paradigm requires that we begin to see multiculturalism as God's creation. Moreover, in light of that desire to see culture as a creation of God, Christians are called to achieve both cultural and cross-cultural competence in order to function effectively in a globalized world.

8

Shalom: A Kingdom Motif for the Educational Setting

THE ESSENTIAL GOAL OF multicultural education is to build a community of shalom. Isaiah 11:6 clearly depicts the image of the community of shalom where the lion and the lamb lie down together. The term *shalom* originally refers to wholeness. It is "the inner wholeness of the fulfilled person, but it is also a relational word including (upward) peace with God, and (outward) peaceful integration within the society of God's people."[1]

In the community of shalom everything exists in the relationships in which God created them. It is a place where all peoples and cultures are linked together in unity and equality. This community is actually modeled in Genesis 1 with the triune God existing in unity and community. The God who created the universe is a perfect community of the Father, Son, and Spirit, devoid of competition and suppression. In Genesis 1:26 the triune God said, "Let *us* [*Elohim*, plural] make man in our image." Hence, shalom is accomplished when we live in right relationship with God, each other, and nature—and going beyond mere tolerance, we take delight in such relationships.[2] God created humankind as male and female in community, and he asks us to enter into fellowship with each other in a harmonious community (shalom). According to Erickson,

---

1. Motyer, *Message of Philippians*, 209.
2. Cardoza-Orlandi, *Mission*; Miller, "The Gospel of Peace."

> There is a common bond among human beings. The doctrine of creation and of the descent of the entire human race from one original pair means that we are all related to one another. . . . if the bond between us is fully understood and acted upon, it should produce a concern and empathy for other people. We will rejoice with those who rejoice and weep with those who weep, even if they are not fellow Christians.[3]

How can we develop a community of shalom? Palmer identifies ten features of public life, which provide key components to build a community of shalom:

1. Strangers meet on common ground.
2. Fear of the stranger is faced and dealt with.
3. Scarce resources are shared and abundance is generated.
4. Conflict occurs and is resolved.
5. Life is given color, texture, drama, a festive air.
6. People are drawn out of themselves.
7. Mutual responsibility becomes evident and mutual aid possible.
8. Options become audible and accountable.
9. Vision is projected and projects are attempted.
10. People are empowered and protected against power.[4]

Raleigh Washington and Glen Keherin articulated the key principles of shalom ministry to include committed relationship (Ruth 1:16), intentionality (Eph 2:14–16), sincerity (John 15:15), sensitivity (Eph 4:15–16), sacrifice (Phil 2:3–4), interdependence (2 Cor 8:12–14), empowerment (2 Cor 8:9), and repentance and forgiveness (2 Cor 5:17–21).[5]

Shalom, therefore, is not merely the absence of conflict, it is the presence of relational wholeness. It is God's command to humans living here and now in a fallen world—a world filled with pain, suffering, and "woundedness"—to love one another. Shalom closely relates to cross-cultural reconciliation in which we seek to heal the wounds of those involved in ethnic

---

3. Erickson, *Introducing Christian Doctrine*, 168.
4. Palmer, *Going Public*.
5. Washington and Keherin, *Breaking Down Walls*.

wars, racial oppression, gender exploitation, and any kind of injustice and violence that harm human communities and/or the environment.[6]

Shalom should be a hope, an aspiration, and a goal for Christian ministers, educators, and teachers to create an environment in which all persons connect, grow, and develop together in the love of Christ. The community of shalom can be built up through two interventions in education: (1) implementing contextualized pedagogy and (2) pursuing educational goals for social justice.

MULTICULTURAL EDUCATION: PRAXIS FOR CONTEXTUALIZED EDUCATION

Education does not happen in a vacuum but takes place in the complex daily realities of human life in the dynamics of interaction with the immediate personal setting as well as the macro environment. In order to facilitate multicultural education effectively in a classroom, teachers must employ effective teaching strategies that align with students' cultures and contexts. For example, Ladson-Billings suggests that linking school culture with home culture and incorporating culturally relevant teaching skills are critical strategies for planning and teaching in a culturally responsive way.[7] The power of Jesus's teaching resulted from his contextualized education. Lee explains why Jesus's teaching was so effective:

> His teaching was casual and contextualized. He did not follow a systematic reaction to situations or a coherent program. However, his teaching was powerful because he always gained his audiences' attention by establishing points of contact with various persons and groups and by his involvement with them. Jesus' teaching was adapted to his audience, and he differentiated the main focus of his teaching based on his audiences' situations and contexts.[8]

Education should be contextualized. Freire criticized the banking methods of education in which the teacher makes deposits and students silently receive, memorize, and repeat what the teacher instructs.[9] In this method, the teacher cannot meet the individual needs of students. Only

---

6. Cardoza-Orlandi, *Mission*, 85.
7. Ladson-Billings, "But That's Just Good Teaching!"
8. Lee, "Jesus' Teaching and Model," 72.
9. Freire, *Pedagogy of the Oppressed*.

when teachers understand students' cultural backgrounds can they design and deliver instruction that meets their diverse needs. Lingenfelter and Lingenfelter suggest that the main task of a teacher is to create a learning context that is familiar to students yet stretches them beyond their previous experiences.[10] Several contextualized pedagogical models have been suggested. For example, based on Jesus's teaching process in the Bible, Lee articulates a model for a contextualized education process that consists of five stages:

1. Inspiring learning by essential questions
2. Facilitating situated learning
3. Exploring hypotheses
4. Encouraging transfer evaluation
5. Transforming society in a community[11]

Ozele suggests a dialogical pedagogy for multicultural education that provides a forum in which questions are formed, raised, and addressed.[12] Ng recommends a process-orientation method as an effective multicultural pedagogy using story, festival, art, music, drama, as well as symbol, image, and metaphor.[13]

Freire explained contextualized education as a dual process: codification and decodification. Codification is a way of gathering information, representing the learner's day-to-day situations in a visual form (such as a photograph, a drawing) or in a word, an abstract form. Learners engage a group (such as a culture circle) in the task of codifying reality into the representations. Decodification refers to a process of analysis through which people perceive relationships between elements of the codification and other experiences in their day-to-day life. While decoding these images and symbols, the learners recognize their own identity through their own words. The codification and decodification is a dynamic and creative process through which the learners generate critical consciousness and are empowered to alter their relations with nature and unjust social realities.[14]

---

10. Lingenfelter and Lingenfelter, *Teaching Cross-Culturally,* 52.
11. Lee, "Jesus' Teaching Model."
12. Ozele, "Envisioning Culturally-Informed Education."
13. Ng, "Impelled toward Multicultural Religious Education."
14. Freire, *Pedagogy of the Oppressed.*

Multiculturalism

The effectiveness of Freire's method results from his emphasis on contextualized learning materials. In the learning process, all learners share, learn, and reflect their experiences based on their contextual realities. He believed that learners perceive the social, economic, and political contradictions and take action against the oppressive elements of reality. When he taught in Brazil, he treated the illiterate peasants as intelligent adults, knowing that they merely lacked the linguistic tools needed for literacy. By engaging in the codification-decodification process, the learners are educated into the fullness of the human conditions. One critical concept for this contextualized teaching method is the culture circle. The culture circle is a discussion group in which all people engage in dialogue about the reasons for their existential situation. In the culture circle, dialogue is the center of the pedagogical process in which learners and teachers are coinvestigators.

How do educators implement a contextualized pedagogy? What conditions or skills do teachers need? First of all, Christian teachers should be aware that all students are different and they bring their diversity to the classroom. Christian teachers need to be conscious about the significant cultural diversity in the classroom that benefits everyone in the classroom throughout the dialogic process.[15] In order to do this, teachers should analyze the hegemonic aspects of culture and set up an action plan in their daily praxis through intercultural citizenship education.

Second, teaching methods and procedures should be modified and differentiated based on students' cultural and social contexts. Culturally contextualized education inspires students to become sensitive to their relationship with their cultural heritage in order to have a basis for understanding others in their cultural environment.[16] Diaz-Rico and Weed identify four components necessary to facilitate culturally responsive education:

1. Respect for students' diversity
2. Working with culturally supported facilitation
3. Sustaining high expectations for all students
4. Marshaling parental and community support for schooling[17]

---

15. Freire, *Teachers as Cultural Workers*.
16. Ozele, "Envisioning Culturally-Informed Education."
17. Diaz-Rico and Weed, *Cross-Cultural Language and Academic Development Handbook*.

Finally, Christian teachers should encourage learners to work collaboratively and cooperatively. Learning is a co-constitutive process that transforms all participants through their actions in community. People learn as they participate and become intimately involved with a community or culture of learning—interacting with the community in order to understand its history, assumptions, and cultural values and rules. Many teachers fail God when they isolate a minority student to a classroom corner to work alone and feel out of place. Christian teachers should model a sense of community within the classroom. In the contextualized learning process, all participants share communal resources together such as routines, words, tools, ways of doing things, stories, gestures, symbols, genres, actions, or concepts that the community has produced.[18]

Christian educators need to understand the students' larger framework and be able to use a variety of approaches, methods, and techniques in their teaching. Contextualized education is designed to broaden learning beyond cognitive understanding and make intentional and intelligent use of specific contexts both as sites of learning and as teaching and learning experiences in and of themselves.[19]

MULTICULTURAL EDUCATION: PRAXIS FOR SOCIAL JUSTICE

As we discussed, the end goal of multicultural education is to build a community of shalom. Shalom is not merely the absence of conflict, but the prevalence of conditions that contribute to human well-being in all its dimensions.[20] Therefore, shalom results when people live together according to God's intention. Some synonymous terms are *blessing, salvation, righteousness,* and *social justice.*[21]

> Shalom depicts the relationship that God establishes and intends for humanity with Himself, other humans and nature. It relates to communion and fulfillment, where the claims and needs of each individual-in-community are satisfied. It is clearly a gift of God and is directly related to His rule and power.[22]

18. Wenger, *Communities of Practice.*
19. Brelsford and Rogers, *Contextualizing Theological Education.*
20. Miller, "The Gospel of Peace."
21. Metzler, "Shalom is the Mission."
22. Ibid., 37.

Multiculturalism

The community of shalom, therefore, is realized throughout society when all individuals live in community with each other, resisting all tendencies toward division, hostility, separation, and prejudice.

Multicultural education is a tool for social justice and shalom. Multicultural education is an intentional intervention by which educational and social inequality and unjust treatment are removed. The primary goal of multicultural education is to reform the schools and other educational institutions so that students from diverse racial, ethnic, and social groups can experience optimum educational opportunities.

> *Multicultural education is an intentional intervention by which educational and social inequality and unjust treatments are removed.*

Multicultural education is a tool for social justice. We need to seek to challenge and remove the inequalities in our society. How does multicultural education lead to social change? Hernandez points out that education is about significant change occurring by providing dynamic teaching, learning environments, and opportunities that reflect the ideals of equity and excellence. This requires that students develop decision making and social action skills so they can take personal, social, and civic actions to make the United States and the world more democratic and humane.[23] Sleeter and Grant criticize the theory-based interventions of multicultural education, which only promote adding diversity in a school or classroom. They advocate multicultural education as facilitating social reconstruction.[24] Students should be aware of the injustice of society and learn how to acquire constructive responses.

Nieto and Bode's formulation of social justice in education has four components. First, it challenges, confronts, and disrupts misconceptions, untruths, and stereotypes that lead to structural inequality and discrimination based on race, social class, gender, and other social and human differences.[25] This means that Christian teachers with a social justice perspective consciously include topics that focus on inequality in the curriculum, and they encourage their students to work for equality and fairness both in and out of the classroom. Second, it means providing all students with the resources necessary to learn to their full potential. Third, it draws on the

---

23. Hernandez, *Multicultural Education*.
24. Sleeter and Grant, *Making Choices for Multicultural Education*.
25. Nieto and Bode, *Affirming Diversity*, 11–12.

talents and strengths that students bring to their education as a foundation for their learning. The last component is creating a learning environment that promotes critical thinking and a support agency for social change.

How does multicultural education seek to challenge and reform the inequalities that exist in our society? Gorski suggests three levels of social change through multicultural education:

1. The transformation of self
2. The transformation of schools and schooling
3. The transformation of society[26]

First, the transformation of self can be accomplished through individual awareness in a teaching and learning setting. To begin this process, multicultural education allows individuals, students, and teachers to critically analyze societal topics in a historical and contemporary context. The main task of teachers is to help learners recognize and reevaluate their own existential context. Through the process of problem posing, reflective thinking, and comparing and contrasting topics, students and teachers discover and grasp the critical relationships and interconnections between diverse groups and social issues.

The role of the Christian teacher is critical. Freire argued that teachers are ultimately accountable for promoting social justice that develops only through critical consciousness.[27] Zinn said that the first thing teachers have to do is make a decision for themselves that they will not be obedient in staying within the boundaries that are usually set by the principals, school administers, and parent-teacher associations.[28] Giroux and McLaren described teachers' roles as transformative intellectuals who combine scholarly reflection and practice in the service of educating students to be thoughtful, active citizens.[29] The educational goal should be global transformation by transformative intellectuals who critically evaluate the world and its processes, including the political and educational institutions that maintain social inequalities.

Second, multicultural education becomes associated with transformation in schools and schooling. Multicultural educators have developed many theories and practices that embrace diverse ethnic groups and minority

---

26. Gorski, *Multicultural Education and the Internet*.
27. Freire, *Pedagogy of the Oppressed*.
28. Zinn, *A People's History of the United States*.
29. Giroux and McLaren, "Teacher Education and the Politics of Engagement."

Multiculturalism

voices. After critically analyzing the curriculum, textbooks, resources, and other materials, several multicultural educators have found out that those materials reinforce the dominant culture while perpetuating stereotypes of minority groups in mainstream society. They also highly recommend including themes about ethnic groups, women, and various linguistic communities in the curriculum. Ladson-Billings developed culturally relevant techniques that include several important multicultural education strategies, including linking school culture with home culture, and incorporating culturally relevant teaching skills.[30]

The last level of social change through multicultural education is the transformation of society. The goal is for society—through these interventions and programs—to progress and advance to be more ethical, moral, and just. Banks's last approach, social action, includes all of the elements of the transformation approach, but adds components that require students to make decisions and take action related to the concept, issue, or problem studied in any unit.[31] The major goals of instruction are to educate students for social critique and social change and to teach them decision making skills. Freire calls this praxis, which refers to reflection and action upon the world in order to transform it. The process of praxis is never ending, but ongoing as long as we live in this society.[32]

CHAPTER SUMMARY

In this chapter we have engaged the idea of multicultural education as praxis for social justice and as praxis for contextualized education. It argues that multicultural education is a tool for justice and social change that works within three broad categories: First is the transformation of self, allowing for individual awareness through teaching and learning. Second, this initiative involves the transformation of schools and schooling. The last consists of the transformation of society, further creating justice and social change.

Across these three levels of change, multicultural education provides insight for the individual and for society that also transforms schools into a more participative and collaborative setting where all students can share, develop, and create learning opportunities together.

---

30. Ladson-Billings, "But That's Just Good Teaching!"
31. Banks, *Cultural Diversity and Education*.
32. Freire, *Pedagogy of the Oppressed*.

9

Multicultural Stories: Exemplars for Life in a Shalom Community

THIS CHAPTER PRESENTS TWO stories that illustrate how possible it is to live the shalom lifestyle in our fallen world. These stories come from the personal experiences and encounters of the two authors of this book. They are presented as exemplars for how God's people can live out the Christian experience amidst the challenges of our fallen world.

JOHN WILSON WALLACE: A LEGACY OF DELIBERATE AFFIRMATION OF THE DIGNITY OF ALL PEOPLE

This story arises from a personal encounter with a regular guy, a Christian man, not a preacher, not a teacher, just a regular Christian, who attempted to live his life for God and for his people. John Wallace would never have imagined that his story would be told for the whole world to know, for he did all he did in his daily encounters with all people without attracting attention to himself. The best way to introduce him is to quote his son's eulogy at his funeral on Sunday March 3, 2013.

> "O Love, That Will Not Let Me Go," the hymn I just played, was one of John's favorites. The love it describes, God's love, is unconditional and beyond what we as humans are capable of. But Dad's love came close. Those who knew him remember that, once his love focused on us, it never wavered or waned; it never gave up

on us, no matter what we did or said or thought about him. Dad's favorite books, pastimes, foods, and sports teams were loved in the same intense, big-hearted way he loved his friends and family.

We saw this every day throughout his life. Here were some of his greatest loves:

First and foremost, John loved his wife Ruth. Throughout the nearly seventy years of their courtship and marriage, she remained the most important presence in his life. At supermarkets, doctor's offices, and restaurants, the people he ran into had to know that this 86-year-old man still had the girlfriend of his youth, and her name was "Ruthie." He shared this with such guileless conviction that they knew it had to be true. The love of Dad for my mother was reaffirmed every morning before breakfast, and every evening on his way to bed, as he took her hand and tenderly kissed it.

Second, he deeply loved his family: his mother and mother-in-law, his children, his grandchildren and great grandchildren, his brothers and cousins, and their families. This love led him to seek to play a significant part in all of our lives, wherever we were and whatever we were doing. Thus, when I joined the Peace Corps and continued in humanitarian work in Africa and Asia for many years, he had to find some way to share in my experiences. And what came out of this was his long and fruitful involvement in the lives of African and Asian students at Fuller Seminary, where he helped them adapt to American culture, find housing, move from one apartment to another, learn to drive, and obtain a driver's license.

Last but not least, Dad had a huge, unquenchable love for people-in-need, no matter who they were, what their situation in life might be, or whether they could ever repay him. Just this morning, when I was looking for something in one of his file cabinets, I happened to see a card with a quote from Frank Laubach in my Dad's handwriting. It said: "if anybody were to ask me how to find God, I should say at once, hunt down the deepest need you can find and forget all about your own comfort while you try to meet that need. Talk to God about it, and He will be there. You will know it." Our home was a crossroads for people-in-need, as well as a staging ground for the delivery of food and other things they could use. I don't think I ever saw him more joyful than when putting together and delivering hundreds of boxes of food at Christmas time. It was this love of people-in-need that informed my father's lifelong passion for progressive political causes. He simply couldn't abide an un-level playing field and always took the side of the "little guy." And he fervently believed that the Church should speak out loud and clear on issues of poverty and discrimination, taking bold action to make our society fairer.[1]

Those were the words of Stephen Wallace, John's only son. Yet, as powerful as they are, they do not fully capture the person of John Wilson Wallace. I tell this story because I knew John personally. I (Chinaka) was the first of Fuller Seminary students that he worked with. John was an embodiment of shalom for the Christian community. He had a commitment to live out his faith, so in his dealings with his fellow human beings he held on to a sacred commitment to respect the dignity of each person, regardless of ethnicity, race, or social stature. He exemplified in simple terms what it means to be a Christian in a polarized world. He refused to be trapped in the baggage of political ideologies, but rather sought ways to affirm the humanity of all people and be an instrument of encouragement to those in need. I saw John attend to the needs of Hispanic immigrants who were struggling to get a driver's license or put food on the table. He was not concerned about their immigration status, but cared more about their human situations and attempted in his caring to introduce them to the one who alone could give them a permanent residency in heaven, Jesus Christ. If all of God's people would approach life in the Christian community with the same mindset, there will be no need for a book on multiculturalism as a shalom motif for the Christian community. This is because the words of the prophet Isaiah would come to life: "'The wolf and the lamb will feed together, and the lion will eat straw like the ox, and dust will be the serpent's food. They will neither harm nor destroy on all my holy mountain,' says the Lord" (Isa 65:25).

WON-JOON YOON: FORGIVENESS A HALLMARK OF THE SHALOM COMMUNITY

On July 4, 1999, Mr. Won-Joon Yoon, an Indiana University student from Korea, was killed while waiting to enter the Korean United Methodist Church located in Bloomington, Indiana, for Sunday worship service. It was around 10:50 a.m., just ten minutes before the worship service started. The assailant was Benjamin Smith, an ex-Indiana University student and a member of the World Church of the Creator, which was one of the largest and most violent hate organizations in the United States. This group

---

1. Wallace, "John Wilson Wallace."

Multiculturalism

teaches hate and advocates a separation of whites from all other races. They have their own holy book, commandments, and forms of worship, but they are narrow-minded, and in many ways, evil.[2]

When Benjamin Smith passed by on the main street to the Korean church, from inside his Ford Taurus, Smith shot Yon-Joon Yoon twice in the back, and then drove away. Won-Joon fell down on the grass just two or three meters away from the church's main entrance. All the Korean worshippers came out, but there was nothing they could do at that critical moment except pray. They laid their hands on Won-Joon's body and began to pray. "God please do not take this man's life. Give your strength to this man. Please do not let him die." They called 911, but the ambulance did not arrive until about twenty minutes later because it was the Fourth of July holiday. The EMS crew took the body in the ambulance and left. The Korean worshippers went back into the sanctuary and prayed again. About ten minutes later, the church received a call from the hospital, Won-Joon had died. This was the last in a hate-crime spree by Smith that spanned two days and two states (Illinois and Indiana). Smith killed two, Won-Joon and Mr. Richt Byrdsong, an African American and the Northwestern University basketball coach, and injured nine people of ethnic minorities, including six orthodox Jewish men and an Asian American couple. Just before he was about to be captured he killed himself.

We do not know why this tragedy happened to a good Christian. It happened on Sunday (the Lord's day) at his church (his holy place), and Won-Joon was a faithful young man. All of Won-Joon's family were devoted Christians in a predominantly Buddhist country. Shin-Ho, Won-Joon's father, has been an elder at a large church in Korea for a long time. When Mr. Shin-Ho Yoon first heard the news, he said, "It was a terrible shock. We couldn't believe it. Never! For a time being, we couldn't talk to each other." The death of a son was especially painful in an Asian culture that values male heirs. Won-Joon was the only son in the family, and had been exempted from Korean military service, which is required of most Korean males.

At first, the Korean church did not know how to deal with this tragedy. All the international students of Indiana University and the local community fell into a deep depression and silence. But something happened in the community after his death. An innocent young man's death brought a significant change to the community as well as in people's hearts. Out

---

2. Working, "Rampage Left Lasting Wounds," 2.

Multicultural Stories: Exemplars for Life in a Shalom Community

of a senseless tragedy, a sense of hope began to rise. The Korean church leadership team put a banner in front of the church wall, saying, "Hate is not the answer, Only God's love is." Then they tried to show God's love and mercy to the community. A thousand voices of love rose up after one act of hate killed a young man whose full potential had yet to be reached. Every church wall was filled with cards, letters, and messages from all around the country. Won-Joon's faithful life was shared by his friends and it gradually touched other international students and the community. Many churches formed prayer circles and continually prayed. Many lives were transformed by the grace of God. What the enemy meant for evil, God in his mercy, used for good. This sad event led the community to begin to confront their diversity through engagement and critical discourse.

At a memorial service several days after Yoon's death, Shin-Ho Yoon declared that he had forgiven the killer and wanted to meet Smith's parents to let them know he did not blame them at all. He delivered a message of peace and healing from God:

> Our Lord has taken my son away. No more do we have to be sorrowful, because he has gone to be with Christ in heaven. . . . The act was committed by a hatemonger. The killer was also a child of God, loved by his own parents. God will be the final judge. God's word is the last. We have to be moral, showing goodness to our neighbors. I want to meet Smith's parents to share a word of reconciliation. They are also victims of hate crime. God loves them. Won-Joon Yoon still loves America. Through his parents, he still loves America.[3]

Seung-ho Park, the uncle of Won-Joon, also delivered a message at Won-Joon Yoon's funeral. "We are listening to his voice now. His voice is clear and loud enough."[4] He said, "in the name of Jesus, I forgive Ben Smith and I love America." Did you hear his voice?

> As a representative of Won-Joon's family, I also forgive Ben Smith who killed my brother in the name of Jesus. Also, I forgive this country which robbed away the hope from my brother in the name of Jesus. Jesus has come to bring love and peace to this earth. All our family are Christians and all our family send the message of love and peace at this time.[5]

3. Ibid.
4. Ibid.
5. Ibid.

Multiculturalism

On July 12, 1999, more than 2,000 people marched from Indiana University auditorium to the Korean United Methodist Church, and Rev. Phil Amerson of the First United Methodist Church, Bloomington, Indiana, represented the community. He said,

> We have come full circle, returning to the place where hate extinguished hope, and we dedicate ourselves to caring for Won-Joon Yoon's legacy of good will. May we now be a uniting community! May we be a Bloomington loving and uniting so that one day we may be a Bloomington loved and a Bloomington united![6]

Shin-Ho Yoon's deep faith continued to impact the community. At a ceremony on the three-year anniversary of Yoon's death, his father said, "I praise God; I glorify God for taking away my son. Because my son was taken, we (the Body of Christ) have gained a lot of beautiful people, all over the world."[7]

Sometimes we do not know why bad things happen to Christians, but we do know that God often uses a terrible tragedy as an opportunity to reach the world and to spread the gospel of Jesus Christ. The city of Bloomington was born again as a hometown for international students. Since then, the churches in Bloomington eagerly reach people and students from other cultures with tender and caring hearts. One church in Bloomington formed a special ministry that helps international students, visitors, and their families develop a loving, personal relationship with Jesus Christ through fellowship and a Christian education programs. Through its programs and services, the church is filled with many international students and their families.

That is God's church where we embrace all people in worship. In the church, all are welcome because all people are God's children. Jesus died on the cross to save all people. In the Old Testament, Israelites were an exclusive people of God. However, the church of the New Testament is deliberately inclusive and universal, uniting Jews and Gentiles. Paul declares in Galatians 3:28, "There is neither Jew nor Gentile, neither slave nor free, nor is there male and female, for you are all one in Christ Jesus." God's plan was not to replace Israel with the church but to add the Gentiles to Israel in order to form the church. Therefore, the church is for all nations. As Isaiah 56:7 says, "my house [now the church] will be called a house of prayer for

---

6. Ibid.
7. Ibid.

all nations." Acts 4:32 clearly shows that the early believers were one in heart and mind. The early church definitely embraced diversity. Look at the beautiful story of what happened in the early church:

> All the believers were one in heart and mind. No one claimed that any of their possessions was their own, but they shared everything they had. With great power the apostles continued to testify to the resurrection of the Lord Jesus. And God's grace was so powerfully at work in them all that there were no needy persons among them. For from time to time those who owned land or houses sold them, brought the money from the sales and put it at the apostles' feet, and it was distributed to anyone who had need. (Acts 4:32–35)

10

Shalom: A Kingdom Motif for the Twenty-first-Century Church

As we approach the end of this book, let us for a moment examine the implications that the current shifts in world politics, business, and communication have for the gospel. How has the church positioned herself to remain relevant in an age of rapid globalization and the convergence of global forces on the whole world?

GLOBALIZATION AND THE TRENDS OF THE TWENTY-FIRST-CENTURY CHURCH

Globalization is the progressive convergence of world economic and sociopolitical interests into one interrelated network. Economically, globalization is the interdependence of world economic structures to the point that positive or negative developments on one end of the world often have a ripple effect on the rest of the world's economic institutions. Politically, government restructuring in one part of the world has effects on both political and economic developments in other parts of the world. If one nation coughs, the others catch the cold. The shaky economies of Cyprus, Greece, Spain, and other European countries in 2012 and 2013 illustrate this new reality.

Globalization is characterized by multinational corporations and global companies, corporations that operate worldwide without limitations by geographic boundaries. These corporations build plants, raise capital,

Shalom: A Kingdom Motif for the Twenty-first-Century Church

and undertake marketing and production activities wherever it is most advantageous to do so. Examples of such companies include British Petroleum (BP), Toyota Motor Corporations, Apple Corporation, Coca-Cola, and many others.[1]

> *The evangelical church of the twenty-first century has yet to position herself as a global enterprise.*

With globalization, business organizations become "stateless." Operations are located without regard to national boundaries. British Petroleum used to be a European-based corporation, but it is no longer. Corporations tend to go wherever the market takes them. This is probably a higher level of the multinationalism that started in the 1960s. It has become a twenty-first-century phenomenon.

William Ouchi coined the phrase "Theory Z," also referred to as the "Japanese management style," to explain the unique corporate culture that is so different than that of corporate America. This theory speaks of an organizational culture that mirrors the Japanese culture in which workers are more participative and capable of performing many and varied tasks that lead to high performance and organizational values. His new theory of management promised to change the way managers and employees alike think about their jobs, their companies, and their working lives. Many attempts have been made to apply Ouchi's Theory Z to U.S. companies. However, it has not led to much success because of the cultural differences involved. Theory Z thrives in Asian (Japanese) environments where work is collective and interdependent, under "family-like" working conditions.[2]

Does this say that Japanese culture is better than American culture? No, not at all! Every culture has its own pros and cons. The difference is not a matter of right or wrong or of degrees of value. Studying differences is a means for giving the same respect to others or other cultures without judging them through our own cultural lenses. Why? All people are created in the image of God and for his glory. Every human being has an inherent dignity and worth. God created us for a purpose. All humans are precious in his sight and he loves us all. Humans are the most loved of his creation, and he knows each one by name. He has even numbered the hairs on our heads (Matt 10:30).

The evangelical church of the twenty-first century has yet to position herself as a global enterprise. We are still functioning as independent and

1. Harris and Moran, *Managing Cultural Differences*.
2. Ouchi, *Theory Z*.

Multiculturalism

fragmented entities with little or no cohesion. If the church of Christ is to accomplish her purpose in the world, she must desire to be a global community. She must become a community of shalom, a community characterized by justice and fairness. It must become a community whose diversity is harnessed as strength for the expansion of the kingdom, rather than seen as a weakness. The church as a community of shalom must have as her overarching commitment the desire to make the kingdoms of this world the kingdom of our God and his Christ. Adding to the four pillars of a community of shalom as shared earlier, the church must be a community with the following elements:

1. Cultural Identity
2. Cross-Cultural Competence
3. Contextualized Gospel
4. Commitment to Social Justice
5. Christ-Centered Identity

Let's take a moment and unpack these concepts.

A Community with Cultural Identity

The twenty-first-century church does not have to be a church devoid of cultural identity and characteristics. The church as a community of shalom has a place for the Chinese church, the Native American church, the Scandinavian church, and what have you. Since we are essentially cultural beings, we can comfortably retain our cultural identities without it being the exclusive defining factor in our identity. These culturally homogenous churches can still function effectively within the larger body of Christ as credible members of the church and as a community of shalom. Paul was writing to the Romans about this shalom community when he told them, "Now, however, I am on my way to Jerusalem in the service of the Lord's people there. For Macedonia and Achaia were pleased to make a contribution for the poor among the Lord's people in Jerusalem. They were pleased to do it, and indeed they owe it to them" (Rom 5:26–27). Regardless of their ethnic differences, the church in Macedonia owed it to the church in Jerusalem to come to their aid in times of need. Ethnicity and race are secondary to salvation in Jesus Christ, which has made us one people. In 1 Peter 2:9–10, we read,

> But you are a chosen people, a royal priesthood, a holy nation, God's special possession, that you may declare the praises of him who called you out of darkness into his wonderful light. Once you were not a people, but now you are the people of God; once you had not received mercy, but now you have received mercy.

The singular tense used in describing the church should scream at us: "*a* chosen people," "*a* royal priesthood," "Once you were not *a* people, but now you are *the* people of God." Mark the definite article, "*the* people of God." The primary emphasis here is on unity and oneness. This should be the character of the twenty-first-century church.

A Community with Cross-Cultural Competence

The twenty-first-century church must be a church that thrives on cultural as well as cross-cultural competence. Many urban churches do include an array of diverse cultures and social experiences, yet some are comfortably functioning as monocultural communities. They are neither receptive nor responsive to the diversity that surrounds them. This is the case with white churches, Asian churches, Hispanic churches, and African American churches. We are comfortable existing as islands, detached from the realities that surround us on all sides. If cultural competence is the ability to function effectively within our social setting, being able to maneuver through the complexities of cultural and worldview differences, the church of the twenty-first-century is not yet culturally competent, and she must strive to be a culturally competent church.

The twenty-first-century church, having been called to make disciples of all nations, must become cross-culturally competent. Our short- and long-term missionaries can no longer go out into the world with the ethnocentrism and cultural bigotry that characterized the nineteenth- and twentieth-century missionary movements. We must distinguish ourselves as better informed and better prepared cross-cultural workers. We must seek to acquire the cultural and linguistic tools necessary not just for survival in foreign lands, but for effective ministry that expands the kingdom of God.

Multiculturalism

A Community with a Contextualized Gospel

The nature of the gospel as preached by the twenty-first-century church must be different from the gospel as preached by our twentieth-century predecessors. In the twentieth century the church in America, was for the most part comfortable with the "Separate but Equal" doctrine of *Plessey v. Ferguson*. Americans lived and worked and learned in cultural cocoons, separated by the lines of race and color. Preachers tailored their messages to suit the itching ears of their congregations, and they spoke of a God created in their own images. Many America missionaries went to Africa, Asia, and Latin America with the false assumption that they were taking God to these heathens, only to arrive there to find out that God was there ahead of them. The twenty-first-century church must preach a gospel that is not only biblical, but also contextual. The gospel must speak to the needs of the twenty-first-century Americans as well as Asians, Africans, and Latin Americans. In the twentieth century, the great evangelist Billy Graham went to an Apartheid South Africa and refused to publicly speak out against Apartheid. The church of the twenty-first-century must do much better by daring to speak truth to power. Our gospel must address our social situations and speak to the hurts and dryness of our social and spiritual environments.

A Community with a Commitment to Social Justice

The twenty-first-century church must be a church that is active in the pursuit of justice and equity in America and the world at large. The church cannot continue to be champions of capitalism at the expense of justice for the down-trodden and destitute. Moses, the great prophet of Israel's deliverance, said in his farewell to the Israelites,

> When you are harvesting in your field and you overlook a sheaf, do not go back to get it. Leave it for the alien, the fatherless and the widow, so the Lord your God may bless you in all the work of your hands. When you beat the olives from your trees, do not go over the branches a second time. Leave what remains for the alien, the fatherless, and the widow. When you harvest the grapes in your vineyard, do not go over the vines again. Leave what remains for the alien, the fatherless, and the widow. Remember that you were slaves in Egypt. (Deut 24:19–22)

Shalom: A Kingdom Motif for the Twenty-first-Century Church

The idea of the free market must be balanced by the idea of fairness and social responsibility. A church does not represent Jesus Christ if it sits idly by while her bank executive members defraud the masses and then pay fat tithes. The twenty-first-century church must not only preach social justice, it must become actively engaged in effecting social justice. Moses said to Israel, "Do not take advantage of a hired man who is poor and needy, whether he is your brother Israelite or an alien living in one of your towns" (Deut 24:14).

The church's commitment to social justice must include advocacy for equal employment opportunities. In his *Church Diversity*, Scott Williams stated that Sunday remains the most segregated day of the week in America.[3] In the same light, can we dare to say that Christian businesses and organizations remain the most segregated work environments in America? The church has remained miles behind the government and non-Christian organizations in providing employment access to people across ethnic lines. We remain mostly comfortable with "our own kind of people." So many Christian organizations integrate only because the law requires them to do so. If we are sons and daughters of the Most High, joint heirs with the Son, why can we not begin to trust ourselves and begin to make it possible for the kingdoms of this world to become the kingdom of our God and his Christ? This should be the character of the shalom community.

A Community with a Christ-Centered Identity

This may yet be the most controversial section of this book. The twenty-first-century church must be a Christocentric church. It must be clearly stated that we are in the end times, when the propensity of many is to water down the faith in the name of political correctness or whatever name it may have. Peter warned the first-century church as follows:

> ... there will be false teachers among you. They will secretly introduce destructive heresies, even denying the sovereign Lord who bought them—bringing swift destruction on themselves. Many will follow their depraved conduct and will bring the way of truth into disrepute. In their greed these teachers will exploit you with fabricated stories. Their condemnation has long been hanging over them, and their destruction has not been sleeping. (2 Pet 2:1–3)

---

3. S. Williams, *Church Diversity*.

Multiculturalism

The goal of this book is not to advocate universalism in doctrine. Our goal is to "conscientize" the church to become the true body of Christ. We cannot be the true body if our gospel is in any way compromised. Paul laid it down clearly for the Corinthian church when he told them that the thrust of the gospel is simply this, "Christ died for our sins according to the scriptures, that he was buried, that he was raised on the third day according to the scriptures, and that he appeared to Peter" (1 Cor 15:3–6). Any deviation from this gospel is a departure from Christ. Any group of believers that opt for such deviation ceases to belong to the kingdom and would not be the community for whom this message is meant.

THE IDEA OF A MULTICULTURAL CHURCH

Starting from the point of its birth on the day of Pentecost, the church was called to be a community of God's people from all nations, tribes, and tongues. The church as a multicultural community should never be questioned as an idea or as a practical reality. The church should be a hospital for ailing souls, regardless of nationality, ethnicity, or skin color. It should be a half-way house for those who have missed their way and are looking to return home to their Lord and maker. Granted that while on this planet earth the church will find its expressions in every community and among every human group that opens the door to the flow of the Holy Spirit among them, the church must not be defined exclusively by culture.

The idea of the church as a multicultural organization suggests that even though local churches may have come into existence within homogeneous human groups and communities, every church so constituted must nevertheless operate with a mindset that any one of God's children from outside that church's initial social or cultural group can come into the church, find full acceptance, and feel at home among God's people. This idea mandates a deliberate and intentional outreach to those who are different from us, who would come into the body and complement our homogeneity with their diversity, thereby making the church on earth a real copy of the church above (Rev 7:9). Once individuals are able to maneuver around the differences of language to ensure effective communication, they should be made to feel at home with other people of God regardless of their ethnicity, nationality, or race.

Paul encourages us to "make every effort to keep the unity of the spirit through the bond of peace" (Eph 4:3). Shalom is not the absence of differences, but the absence of division. In the community of shalom we embrace one another regardless of ethnic background, socioeconomic status, and cultural differences. We are one unique spiritual body. The individuals never lose their uniqueness or distinctiveness; they never lose their identity. But they do surrender their lives of sin for Christ's righteousness, their intolerance toward specific people and ideas for Christ's embrace. Let us see diversity through God's eyes. It should feel good to see others who are different from us. It should feel good to make friends with people who come from far away from our own cultures. We are one body, with one Spirit, one hope, one Lord, one faith, one baptism, and one God (Eph 4:4–6).

11

Taking the Steps Towards a Multicultural Community

THE JOURNEY TOWARDS A multicultural community is an intentional journey. It cannot just happen. There is a difference between a diverse group gathering together and a multicultural community where each member feels like he or she belongs. Many years ago while attending Fuller Theological Seminary in Pasadena, I (Chinaka) attended a large church in Pasadena with people from many parts of the world in it. We congregated on Sunday mornings to worship and dispersed after the wonderful service of powerful word and music. No real effort was made to pull these worshippers into a real community of God's people, yet the church prided itself in having all kinds of people in her congregation. I have also had the privilege of working for a while in a Christian college, and the intentionality towards building a multicultural community at this college has been rather more positive and more obvious. Multicultural communities of God's people are deliberate and focused on making the sense of community a reality. This concluding chapter discusses the stages through which a Christian community can develop multiculturalism.

STAGE ONE: STAGE OF CULTURAL SELF-AWARENESS

Just as each of us needs to go through a stage of self-reflection and soul searching regarding our cultural identity and cultural competency, any church or Christian college, or any other Christian community that desires to be multicultural must take time to reflect on who they are as a community. For example, I once belonged to an all-white Southern Baptist church in Pasadena, California. The church was started in the 1940s for Southerners who had migrated to California to settle there. As a Southern Baptist church planted in the west, for many years the members shared ethnic, class, and educational similarities. It was a place where people went to meet others who shared common characteristics, who also believed in the Lord Jesus with a conservative doctrinal conviction.

Over the years, Pasadena changed. What used to be a Caucasian community became a community of Armenians, Hispanics, African Americans, Asians, and Arabs. While the community changed, the church remained the same. As the population that made up the church began to move away due to economic opportunities in other places or pass away due to old age, the church began to dwindle numerically. Over time, the only new people that came to the church would be international students with a Baptist background who came to study at Fuller Theological Seminary or people who came to work at the U.S. Center for World Mission.

A time came when the church realized that it had to rethink its purpose for the present day Pasadena. It may have served a different purpose since its founding, but to remain a viable body of faith, it had to rethink its mission and purpose and decide whether to remain who it had been or retool to meet the needs of the contemporary setting. This rethinking led to the emergence of a multicultural church. Every church, Christian college, and other Christian community of twenty-first-century America must ask itself the questions, Who are we? What is our purpose in this immediate community? And what is our purpose for the world at large? If the Christian community determines that it would better accomplish her purpose in the community by remaining homogenous, that's fine. Not every Christian community needs to become multicultural, especially if the community does not have much diversity. A church in rural Iowa does not have to be multicultural, unless her population demographics change and God brings along people who may be different who need to be reached with the gospel. Every church must define its place and purpose within the plan of God for the world. Christian colleges, however, may not have that luxury. A combination of students' tendency to go to college anywhere they choose and the many federal government mandates make this choice almost impossible, so Christian colleges cannot afford to avoid diversity.

STAGE TWO: STAGE OF MULTICULTURAL AWARENESS

At this stage the Christian community begins to take a purposeful look at her constituents. How has our neighborhood changed in comparison to our Christian community? Who are our constituents today? Who are our prospects? In the case of a church, do we have people in the church's vicinity who have to go outside the neighborhood to worship simply because they are different from the people in our church? Does our church attract people who are different from us due to our prestige, fame, architecture, or other appeals? For colleges, does our institution attract people who are different from the majority population? Why or why not?

The next question is, How have we responded to these people who are different from us? How have we reached out to them in the community? How have we welcomed them when they have visited or tried to join our community? Do we have any structured program for recognizing them and working hard to get them integrated into our community? More often than not, the answers to these questions reveal significant weaknesses on the side of the Christian community. This process is usually painful and hard to confront. It reveals the institution's ethnocentrism and narrow focus.

Most United States communities are undergoing demographic changes, even in rural Iowa, just mentioned. The Christian community needs to become alive to these changes and plan to respond to them. As time goes by, it will become more and more pressing that Christian communities take the time to identify where they are headed and begin to invest in the shaping of their community to become a welcoming place (house of prayer) for all people, not just the people who look like us. Every church, Christian college, and Christian community must become relevant to the context in which it has been placed, and at the same time receptive to people who may be different yet who are attracted to her.

STAGE THREE: STAGE OF DECISION AND PLANNING TOWARDS A MULTICULTURAL COMMUNITY

Once the Christian community has determined her purpose in the world and has come to realize that she needs to position herself to become relevant to the community in which she has been located, then she will need to make plans for achieving that goal. Existing members of the community must be taken along on the journey towards multiculturalism. Much effort and energy must be expended to educate the constituents and prepare them to become open and receptive to God's children who may be different from them. If we fail to do this all-important job, we will go out and bring people in only to turn them away in bitterness because they have been brought into a community that was not prepared for or ready to be receptive to them.

Structured and targeted planning for reaching the diverse groups in the community is the next step. This outreach must be led by individuals who are one hundred percent sold on the idea of a multicultural community. The institution's policy and practice, along with its position on diversity, need to be published in literature that can be easily handed to people in the community who are different.

Follow-up, orientation, and integration is another critical step in this planning process. Clear and specific plans must be made on how to receive these individuals into the community, how to follow-up with them once they show up, and how to integrate them into active involvement through service and leadership in the community.

STAGE FOUR: STAGE OF INVESTMENT AND IMPLEMENTATION

A critical review of the plan will reveal the need for the investment of money and human resources into building a multicultural community. Producing the relevant literature for outreach and follow-up requires money. Orientation and integration require the investment of money and personnel to provide the needed support to these new people.

The journey towards building a multicultural community requires much investment of human resources as well as money. There must be committed individuals to do the outreach. There must be committed individuals to welcome the new people. There must also be committed people to do follow-up until these individuals are integrated into the community.

Building a multicultural community is not a single short-term project, activity, or event. It is a long-term commitment. The Christian community must have a standing team (not one person) who oversees the process, do the planning and implementation, and make time to collect data on activities and results. The collected data must be closely examined, and the positive and negative issues that emerge be reflected upon and decisions made about correcting errors and enhancing successful activities.

STAGE FIVE: STAGE OF REFLECTION, RETOOLING, AND REINVESTING

Building a multicultural community calls for constant retooling and ongoing investment of human and financial resources. It calls for constant data collection: the new people, who would certainly be a minority at the beginning, need avenues to express their frustrations and disappointments so the Christian community can recognize them and take the necessary steps to address the concerns. Data should also be collected from original members on how the new dynamic is affecting their own sense of belonging to the community.

There must be constant dialogue and exchange in order for the dream to become a reality. It will take a long time before everyone involved adjusts to the reality of this new community. It takes a long time before the benefits of a multicultural community becomes real to all involved. A sad reality is that the Christian community must be prepared to lose some previous constituents who will not be able to handle the change and will look somewhere else for the familiar community they were used to. This is part of the collateral damage that accompanies building a multicultural community, but when the true community is built, it will see the loss as worthwhile.

STAGE SIX: STAGE OF ACCOMPLISHMENT

How long does it take to get to this stage of accomplishing a multicultural community? No one can say. It depends entirely on the setting. It happens faster in some communities than in others. You know this stage has been reached when both the constituents and the institutional leadership begin to reflect a unified face of diversity. You reach it when the fellowship among the constituents, outside of the institution, begins to reflect a diverse and integrated fellowship. Birthdays and wedding anniversaries, Super Bowl Sundays, and the like are enjoyed together in communal celebration of God's people from different cultures and races, joined by the common bond of love and the blood of Jesus.

When a community gets to this point, it presents a model for others to follow. This has nothing to do with the size of the organization; rather, it has everything to do with the size of their faith in Christ: "if you have faith and do not doubt, . . . you can say to this mountain, 'Go, throw yourself into the sea,' and it will be done" (Matt 21:21).

Bibliography

Adams, Daniel J. "Towards a Theological Understanding of Postmodernism." *Cross Currents* 47, no. 4 (Winter 1997/98): 518–30.
Agyeman, Julian. "Steps to Becoming Culturally Competent Communicators." *Human Nature* 6, no. 2 (October 2001): 1–2, http://www.barrfoundation.org/usr_doc/steps_to_becoming_culturally_competent_communicators.pdf.
Aldrich, Joseph C. *Life-Style Evangelism: Learning to Open Your Life to Those Around You.* Portland, OR: Multnomah Press. 1981.
Althusser, Louis. *Lenin and Philosophy and Other Essays.* New York: Monthly Review Press, 2001.
Apple, Michael. *Education and Power.* Boston: Routledge & Keagan, 1982.
Atkinson, Donald R, George Morten, and Derald W. Sue, eds. *Counseling American Minorities: A Cross Cultural Perspective.* 5th ed. Boston: McGraw Hill, 1998.
Atwater, A. A. "An Investigation of Teacher's Color-Blind Racial Attitudes and Diversity Training Experiences: Implications for Teacher Education." *Journal of Education and Human Development* 1, no. 2 (2007): 1–15.
Banks, James A. *Cultural Diversity and Education: Foundations, Curriculum, and Teaching.* Boston: Allyn & Bacon, 2001.
———. "Teaching for Social Justice, Diversity, and Citizenship in a Global World." *The Education Forum* 68 (2004): 289–97.
———. *Teaching Strategies for Ethnic Studies.* 8th ed. Boston: Pearson Education, 2009.
Banks, James A., and Cheryl McGee Banks. *Handbook of Research on Multicultural Education.* San Francisco: John Wiley & Sons, 2004.
———. *Multicultural Education: Issues and Perspectives.* 6th ed. New York: John Wiley & Sons, 2007 [1st ed. 1989; 8th ed. 2013].
Bate, Stuart C. "The Church and the Culture of the Networked World." *Journal of Theology for Southern Africa* 121 (March 2005): 19–33.
Berkowitz, Peter. "Constitutional Conservatism." *Policy Review* 153 (2009): 3–23.
Bernstein, Basil. *Class, Codes and Control.* London: Routledge & Keagan, 1976.
Berryman, Phillip. *Liberation Theology: The Essential Factors about the Revolutionary Movement in Latin America and Beyond.* New York: Pantheon, 1987.
Bourdieu, Pierre. "The Forms of Cultural Capital." In *Handbook of Theory and Research for Sociology of Education*, edited by John G. Richardson, 241–58. New York: Greenwood Press, 1986.
Boutte, Gloria. *Multicultural Education: Raising Consciousness.* Belmont, CA: Wadsworth, 1999.

Bibliography

Bowles, Samuel, and Herbart Gintis. *Schooling in Capitalist America*. New York: Basic Books, 1976.

Breslford, Theodore, and P. Alice Rogers, eds. *Contextualizing Theological Education*. Cleveland, OH: Pilgrim Press, 2008.

Bright, John. *The Kingdom of God*. Nashville: Abingdon, 1981.

Brown, Phil. *Toward a Marxist Psychology*. San Francisco: Harper & Row, 1974.

Burnett, David G. *The Healing of the Nations: Biblical Basis of the Mission of God*. Carlisle, Cumbria: Paternoster, 1996.

Cannan, Joyce. "Developing a Pedagogy of Critical Hope." *Learning and Teaching in the Social Sciences* 2, no. 3 (2005): 159–74.

Cardoza-Orlandi, Carlos. *Mission: An Essential Guide*. Nashville: Abingdon, 2002.

Chege, Mwangi. "Literacy and Hegemony: Critical Pedagogy vis-à-vis Contending Paradigms." *International Journal of Teaching and Learning in Higher Education* 21, no. 2 (2009): 228–38.

Colson, Charles, and Nancy Pearcey. *How Now Shall We Live?* Wheaton, IL: Tyndale House, 1999.

"Conservative vs. Liberal Beliefs." StudentNewsDaily.com, copyright 2005, revised 2010, http://www.studentnewsdaily.com/conservative-vs-liberal-beliefs/.

Cross, Terry, Barbara Bazron, K. W. Dennis, and Mareasa R. Isaac. *Toward a Culturally Competent System of Care*. Washington, DC: Georgetown University Development Center, 1989.

Cuzzort, Raymond Paul, and Edith W. King. *Humanity and Modern Social Thought*. Hinsdale, IL: The Dryden Press, 1976.

Devine, Sean. "Christianity, Science, and Postmodernism." *Stimulus* 15, no. 1 (2007): 28–33.

Diaz-Rico, Lynne T., and Katheryne Weed. *The Cross-Cultural Language and Academic Development Handbook: A Complete K-12 Reference Guide*. 3rd ed. Boston: Allyn & Bacon, 2006.

Diller, Jerry, and Jean Moule. *Cultural Competence: A Primer for Educators*. Belmont, CA: Thomson/Wadsworth, 2005.

DomNwachukwu, Chinaka Samuel. *An Introduction to Multicultural Education: From Theory to Practice*. Lanham, MD: Rowman & Littlefield, 2010.

———. "Through the Eyes of Faith: The Mandate of Teacher Goodness." In *Doing Good and Departing from Evil*, edited by Carol Lambert. New York: Peter Lang, 2009.

Doorly, William J. *Prophet of Justice: Understanding the Book of Amos*. New York: Paulist Press, 1989.

Dreher, Rod. *Crunchy Cons: The New Conservative Counterculture and Its Return to Roots*. New York: Three Rivers Press, 2006.

D'Souza, Dinesh. *Illiberal Education: The Politics of Race and Sex on Campus*. New York: Free Press, 1991.

Egner, David C. "Cutting a Trial." *Daily Bread*. Grand Rapids, MI: Radio Bible Class Ministries, April 24, 2012.

Eichrodt, Walther. *Man in the Old Testament*. London: SCM, 1951.

Elmer, Duane. *Cross-Cultural Conflict: Building Relationships for Effective Ministry*. Downers Grove, IL: InterVarsity Press, 1993.

Erickson, Millard J. *Introducing Christian Doctrine*. 2nd ed. Grand Rapids, MI: Baker Academic, 2001.

Ferdman, Bernardo, and Gabriel Horenczyk. "Cultural Identity and Immigration: Reconstructing the Group during Cultural Transition." In *Language, Identity and Immigration*, edited by Elite Olshtain and Gabriel Horenczyk, 81–100. Jerusalem: Hebrew University Magnes Press, 2000.

Ferm, Deane Willa. *Contemporary American Theologies: A Critical Survey*. New York: Seabury Press, 1981.

Freire, Paulo. *Pedagogy of the Oppressed*. Translated by Myra Ramos [1970]. New York. Herder & Herder, 1972.

———. *The Politics of Education: Culture, Power, and Liberation*. Westport, CT: Bergin & Garvey, 1985.

———. *Teachers as Cultural Workers: Letters to Those Who Dare Teach*. Boulder, CO: Westview Publishers, 1998.

Frey, Christopher. "The Impact of the Biblical Idea of Justice on Present Discussions of Social Justice." In *Justice and Righteousness: Biblical Themes and their Influences*, edited by Henning G. Reventflow and Yair Hoffman. Sheffield, England: JSOT Press, 1992.

Gardner, Morgan, and Deborah Florence Toope. "A Social Justice Perspective on Strength-Based Approaches: Exploring Educators' Perspectives and Practices." *Canadian Journal of Education* 34, no. 3 (2011): 86–102.

Garry, Patrick M. "A Turning Point for Modern Conservatism." *Modern Age* 49, no. 1 (2007): 24–36.

Gi, Jie. "Postmodernism and Marxism: What Is Called into Question in the Educational Discourse?" Paper presented at the Annual Meeting of the American Educational Research Association, Chicago, IL, March 24–28, 1997.

Giroux, Henry A. "Democracy, Education, and Politics of Critical Pedagogy." *Critical Pedagogy: Where Are We Now?*, edited by Peter McLaren and Joe L. Kincheloe. New York: Peter Lang, 2007.

———. *Teachers as Intellectuals: Toward a Critical Pedagogy of Learning*. South Hadley: Bergin & Garvey, 1988.

Giroux, Henry, and Peter McLaren. "Teacher Education and the Politics of Engagement: The Case for Democratic Schooling." In *Breaking Free: The Transformative Power of Critical Pedagogy*, edited by Pepi Leistyna, Arlie Woodrum, and Stephen A. Sherlom, 301–31. Cambridge, MA: Harvard Educational Review, 1996.

Glasser, Arthur F., Charles Van Engen, Dean S. Gilliland, and Shawn B. Redford. *Announcing the Kingdom*. Grand Rapids, MI: Baker Academic, 2003.

Gollnick, Donna, and Philip Chinn. *Multicultural Education in a Pluralistic Society*. Upper Saddle River, NJ: Pearson, 2009.

Gomperz, Theodore. *Greek Thinkers: A History of Ancient Philosophy*. Vol. 1. London: John Murray, 1964.

Gorski, Paul. *Multicultural Education and the Internet: Intersection and Integrations*. 2nd ed. Boston: McGraw-Hill, 2005.

Gottesman, Isaac. "Sitting in the Waiting Room, Paulo Freire and the Critical Turn in the Field of Education." *Educational Studies* 46 (2010): 376–99.

Graham, Donovan L. *Teaching Redemptively: Bringing Grace and Truth into Your Classroom*. Colorado Springs, CO: Purposeful Design, 2003.

Greene, Maxine. *The Dialectics of Freedom*. New York: Teachers College Press, 1988.

Haddad, Daphne W. "And Who Is My Neighbor: Multicultural Education Challenges Christian Educators." In *Nurturing and Reflective Teachers: A Christian Approach for*

Bibliography

the 21st Century, edited by Daniel C. Elliott and Stephen D. Holtrop. Washington, DC: Learning Light Educational Consulting and Publications, 1999.

Haidt, Jonathan. "Born This Way?" *Reason* 44, no. 1 (2012): 24–33.

Ham, Ken, and Charles Ware. *One Race, One Blood: A Biblical Answer to Racism*. Green Forest, AR: Master Books, 2010.

Harris, Philip R., and Robert T. Moran. *Managing Cultural Differences*. Houston, TX: Gulf Professional Publishing, 1999.

Haught, Nancy. "Former Multnomah U. President 'Dr. Joe' Aldrich Dies." *The Oregonia*, http://www.oregonlive.com/news/index.ssf/2009/02/former_multnomah_university_pr.html.

Hasel, Gerhard F. *Understanding the Book of Amos*. Grand Rapids, MI: Baker Book House, 1991.

Helms, Janet, and Donelda Cook. *Using Race and Culture in Counseling and Psychotherapy: Theory and Process*. Columbus, OH: Merrill, 1999.

Hernandez, Hilda. *Multicultural Education: A Teacher's Guide to Linking Context, Process, and Content*. 2nd ed. Columbus, OH: Merrill, 2001.

Hesselgrave, David J. *Communicating Christ Cross-Culturally: An Introduction to Missionary Communication*. 2nd ed. Grand Rapids, MI: Zondervan, 1991.

Hesselgrave, David J., and Edward Rommen. *Contextualization: Meanings, Methods, and Models*. Grand Rapids, MI: Baker Book House, 1989.

Hooks, Bell. *Teaching to Transgress*. New York: Routledge, 1994.

Hytten, Kathy, and Silvia C. Bettez. "Understanding Education for Social Justice." *Educational Foundations* 25 (Winter-Spring 2011): 7–24.

"Irving Kristol: The Man Who Put 'Neo' into Conservatism." *Wall Street Journal*, September 9, 2009.

"John L. O'Sullivan on *Manifest Destiny*, 1839." Excerpted from "The Great Nation of Futurity." *The United States Democratic Review* 6, no. 23 (1839): 426–30. Available at https://www.mtholyoke.edu/acad/intrel/osulliva.htm.

Jones, Jeffrey M. "In U.S., Democrats Re-Establish Lead in Party Affiliation." Gallup Politics, January 9, 2013, http://www.gallup.com/poll/159740/democrats-establish-lead-party-affiliation.aspx.

Joldersma, Clarence W. "Introduction" to *Educating for Shalom: Essays on Christian Higher Education*, by Nicholas Wolterstorff. Grand Rapids, MI: Eerdmans, 2004.

Joldersma, Clarence W., and Gloria G. Stronks. "Preface" to *Educating for Shalom: Essays on Christian Higher Education*, by Nicholas Wolterstorff. Grand Rapids, MI: Eerdmans, 2004.

"Justice." *The Microsoft Encarta Dictionary*. New York: St. Martin's Press, 2001.

Knight, George R. *Philosophy and Education: An Introduction in Christian Perspective*. 4th ed. Berrien Springs, MI: Andrew University Press, 2006.

Koppelman, Kent L., and R. Lee Goodhart. *Understanding Human Differences: Multicultural Education for a Diverse America*. Boston: Pearson, 2005 [1st ed.].

Kowalski, Charles. "Three Dimensions of Cultural Identity." In *The 28th Annual International Conference on Language Teaching and Learning Proceedings*, 256–63. Shizuoka, Japan, 2002.

Kozol, Jonathan. *The Shame of the Nation: The Restoration of Apartheid Schooling in America*. New York: Crown, 2005.

Kraft, Charles H. *Christianity in Culture: A Study in Dynamic Biblical Theologizing in Cross-Cultural Perspective*. New York: Orbis, 1998.

Ladson-Billings, Gloria. "But That's Just Good Teaching! The Case for Culturally Relevant Pedagogy." *Theory Into Practice* 34 (1995): 159–65.

Lasor, William Sanford, David Alan Hubbard, and Frederic William Bush. *Old Testament Survey*. Grand Rapids, MI: Eerdmans, 1996.

Lee, Heekap. "Building a Community of Shalom: What the Bible Says about Multicultural Education." *International Community of Christians in Teacher Education Journal* 5, no. 2 (2010).

———. "Jesus' Teaching and Model and Its Embedded Constructivist Principles." In *Faith-Based Education that Constructs: A Creative Dialogue between Constructivism and Faith-Based Education*, edited by Heekap Lee. Eugene, OR: Wipf and Stock, 2010.

Leonhard, Wolfgang. *Three Faces of Marxism: The Political Concepts of Soviet Ideology, Maoism, and Humanist Marxism*. Translated by Ewald Osers. New York: Holt, Rinehart & Winston, 1974.

Levin, Yuval. "Responses to Wilfred McClay." *First Things*, May 2012.

Lingenfelter, Judith E., and Sherwood G. Lingenfelter. *Teaching Cross-Culturally: An Incarnational Model for Learning and Teaching*. Grand Rapids, MI: Baker Academic, 2003.

Macchia, F. D. "Babel and the Tongues of Pentecost: Reversal or Fulfillment? A Theological Perspective." In *Speaking in Tongues: Multi-disciplinary Perspectives*, edited by Mark J. Cartledge. Milton Keynes, UK: Paternoster, 2006.

Matthew Henry's Bible Commentary on the Whole Bible. Vol. 1: *Genesis to Deuteronomy*. Peabody, MA: Hendrickson, 1991.

Marshall, Chris. *The Little Book of Biblical Justice*. Intercourse, PA: Good Books, 2005.

McClay, Wilfred M. "Liberalism after Liberalism." *First Things*, May 2012.

McGavran, Donald. *Christianity and Cultures*. Washington, DC: Canon, 1974.

McLaren, Peter. *Life in Schools: An Introduction to Critical Pedagogy in the Foundation of Education*. New York: Longman, 1989.

———. "Multiculturalism and the Post-Modern Critique: Towards a Pedagogy of Resistance and Transformation." In *Between Borders: Pedagogy and the Politics of Cultural Studies*, edited by Henry A. Giroux and Peter McLaren. New York: Routledge, 1994.

McLaren, Peter, and Ramin Farahmandpur. *Teaching against Global Capitalism and the New Imperialism: A Critical Pedagogy*. Lanham, MD: Rowman & Littlefield, 2005.

Mcllory, David. *A Biblical View of Law and Justice*. Waynesboro, GA: Paternoster, 2004.

Metzler, James E. "Shalom Is the Mission." In *Mission and the Peace Witness*, edited by Robert L. Ramseyer, 36–51. Scottdale, PA: Herald Press. 1979.

Miller, Merlin. "The Gospel of Peace." In *Mission and the Peace Witness*, edited by Robert L. Ramseyer, 9–23. Scottdale, PA: Herald Press. 1979.

Minanmi, Masachiko, and Carlos J. Ovando. "Language Issues in Multicultural Contexts." In *Handbook of Research on Multicultural Education*, edited by James Banks and Cheryl McGee-Banks. San Francisco: John Wiley & Sons, 2004.

Motyer, J. Alec. *The Message of Philippians*. The Bible Speaks Today. Leicester, England: Inter-Varsity Press, 1984.

Nardoni, Enrique. *Rise Up, O Judge: A Study of Justice in the Biblical World*. Peabody, MA: Hendrickson, 2004.

Nash, Gary. "Multiculturalism and History: Historical Perspectives and Present Prospects." In *Historical Perspectives on the Current Education Reforms*, edited by Diane Ravitch

Bibliography

and Maris Vinovskis. Essays commissioned by the Office of Research (OR) in the Office of Educational Research and Improvement (OERI), U.S. Department of Education, 1993.

Newton, Jon. "The Challenge of Postmodernity." In *Pointing the Way: Directions for Christian Education in a New Millennium*, edited by J. Ireland, 175–200. Australia: National Institute for Christian Education, 2004.

Ng, David. "Impelled toward Multicultural Religious Education." *Religious Education* 87, no. 2 (1992): 192–202.

Niebuhr, Reinhold. *Christ and Culture*. New York: Harper & Row, 1951.

———. *The Nature and Destiny of Man: A Christian Interpretation*. Vol. 2. New York: Charles Scribner's Sons, 1964.

Nieto, Sonia. "School Reform and Student Learning: A Multicultural Perspective." In *Multicultural Education: Issues and Perspectives*, edited by James A. Banks and Cherry McGee-Banks, 401–20. New York: John Wiley & Sons, 2005.

Nieto, Sonia, and Patty Bode. *Affirming Diversity: The Sociopolitical Context of Multicultural Education*. 5th ed. Boston: Pearson Education, 2008.

NIV Encouragement Bible. Grand Rapids, MI: Zondervan, 2001.

Noebel, David, and Chuck Edwards. *Thinking Like a Christian*. Nashville: B & H Publishing, 2002.

Norton, Delores G. *Dual Perspectives: The Inclusion of Ethnic Minority Content in Social Work Curriculum*. New York: Council on Social Work Education, 1978.

O'Sullivan, John L. "The Great Nation of Futurity." *The United States Democratic Review* 6, no. 23 (July-August 1845): 426–30.

Ouchi, William G. *Theory Z: How American Business Can Meet the Japanese Challenge*. Reading, MA: Addison-Wesley, 1981.

Ozele, Anthony M. "Envisioning Culturally-Informed Education." Paper presented at the Annual Meeting of the Religious Education Association, Oberlin, OH, November 3–5, 2006.

Palmer, Parker. *Going Public*. Washington, DC: The Alban Institute, 1980.

Panikulam, George. *Koinonia in the New Testament: A Dynamic Expression of Christian Life*. Rome: Biblical Institute Press, 1979.

Quinn, Justin. "What Are the Different Types of Conservatives?" On About.com. US Conservative Politics Web site: http://usconservatives.about.com/od/conservativepolitics101/tp/Are-You-A-Conservative-.htm (October 10, 2012).

Reich, Robert Bernard. *Education and the Next Economy*. Washington, DC: National Education Association, 1988.

Riseberg, D. F. "Framework and Foundations: Setting the Stage and Establishing Norms." Paper presented at the first National Conference on Human Relations, Minneapolis, MN, June 18, 1978.

Russell, Letty M. *The Future of Partnership*. Philadelphia: Westminster Press, 1979.

Savery, John R., and Thomas M. Duffy. "Problem Based Learning: An Instructional Model and Its Constructivist Framework." *Educational Technology* 35, no. 5 (1995): 31–38.

Schneider, Isidor. "Introduction" to *The Enlightenment: The Culture of the Eighteenth Century*, edited by Isidor Schneider. New York: George Braziller, 1965.

Slater, Thomas. "Justice." *The Catholic Encyclopedia*. Vol. 8. New York: Robert Appleton, 1910. Online edition: 28 July 2013, http://www.newadvent.org/cathen/08571c.htm.

Sleeter, Christine E., and Carl A. Grant. *Making Choices for Multicultural Education: Five Approaches to Race, Class, and Gender*. New York: John Wiley & Sons, 2003.

Bibliography

Snyder, Howard A. *A Kingdom Manifesto*. Downers Grove, IL: InterVarsity Press, 1985.

———. *Models of the Kingdom*. Eugene, OR: Wipf and Stock, 1991.

Sproul, Robert Charles. *Lifeviews*. Grand Rapids, MI: Revell, 1986.

Standish, Paul. "Social Justice in Translation: Subjectivity, Identity, and Occidentalism." *Educational Studies in Japan: International Year Book* 6 (December 2011): 69–79.

Steinberg, Shirley R. "Where Are We Now?" In *Critical Pedagogy: Where Are We Now?*, edited by Peter McLaren and Joe L. Kincheloe. New York: Peter Lang, 2007.

Strassberg, Barbara A. "Magic, Religion, Science, Technology, and Ethics in the Postmodern World." *Zygon* 40, no. 2 (June 2005): 307–22.

"Text: George Bush's Speech to the NAACP." July 10, 2000. *Washington Post*, On Politics Web site: http://www.washingtonpost.com/wp-srv/onpolitics/elections/bushtext071000.htm.

Toulmin, Stephen. *The Return to Cosmology: Postmodern Science and the Theology of Nature*. Berkeley: University of California Press, 1982.

Unger, Merrill, F. *New Testament Teaching on Tongues*. Grand Rapids, MI: Kregel, 1971.

Wallace, Stephen. "John Wilson Wallace." Eulogy presented at the First Church of the Nazarene, Pasadena, California, Sunday March 3, 2013.

Washington, Raleigh, and Glen Keherin. *Breaking Down Walls*. Chicago: Moody Press, 1993.

Wenger, Etienne. *Communities of Practice: Learning, Meaning, and Identity*. New York: Cambridge University Press, 1998.

Williams, George Washington. *History of the Negro Race in America from 1619 to 1880*. New York: G.P. Putnam's Sons, 1883.

Williams, Scott. *Church Diversity*. Green Forest, AR: New Leaf Press, 2011.

Willis, Richard W., Sr. *Martin Luther King, Jr. and the Image of God*. Oxford: Oxford University Press, 2009.

Working, Russell. "Rampage Left Lasting Wounds." *Chicago Tribune*, July 4, 2004, p. 2.

Wolters, Albert M. *Creation Regained: Biblical Basics for a Reformational Worldview*. Grand Rapids, MI: Eerdmans, 1985.

Wolterstorff, Nicholas. *Educating for Shalom: Essays on Christian Higher Education*. Grand Rapids, MI: Eerdmans, 2004.

Yoder, Perry. *Shalom: The Bible's Word for Salvation, Justice, and Peace*. Nappanee, IN: Evangel Publishing House, 1987.

Young, Iris Marion. "Five Faces of Oppression." In *Readings for Diversity and Social Justice*, edited by Maurianne Adams, Warren J. Blumenfield, Carmelita Castaneda, and Heather W. Hackman, 35–49. New York: Routledge, 2000.

Zinn, Howard. *A People's History of the United States 1492-Present*. San Francisco: HarperCollins, 2003.

Index

ability, 56, 69–70, 72, 90, 100–101, 105–6, 131
abortion, 8, 10, 12–14
abraham, 19, 61, 74, 77–82, 86–87, 94, 107
Abram, 74–75, 77–78, 87, 92
acculturation process, 103
acts, 4, 24, 69, 81–83, 88–89, 107, 127
adaptation, 27–28, 36, 71, 106
Agyeman, Julian, 106, 141
aldrich, 16, 26–29, 141, 144
alienation, 97
aliens, 79, 109
Althusser, Louis, 34, 141
american history, 44, 51–52
american schools, 50–51, 53
american subcultures, 7
American (s)
  christianity, 4
  church, 90–91, 130–131
  classrooms, 54
  culturte, 122, 129
  democracy, 5
  evangelicals, 1, 68
  latin, 43
  native, 52
  people, 7, 9
  values, 6–7
America's purpose, 91
America's racism, 78–79
Amos, 62, 63, 108–9, 142, 144
ancestry, 69, 103
Anglo-Saxon, 7, 26
animals, 20, 66–67, 74–76
anthropology, 23

anti-christian, 19, 28, 40, 50
apostles, 91, 127
Arabic numerals, 51
ark, 75–76, 82, 85
Asia, 81–82, 93, 109, 122, 124, 129, 132
attitudes, racial, 55, 106, 141
attributes, 32, 67, 77
Atwater, A.A, 106, 141
authorities, 20, 22
awareness, 7, 100–101, 105–6
  critical, 42
  cultural, 56
  individual, 119–20
  multicultural, 138

Babel, 71–74
Banks , 15, 31, 35, 46, 51–52, 55, 104–5, 120
  James, 35, 51, 54, 104, 141, 145–46
  McGee, 15, 31, 35, 46, 55, 141, 145–46
beasts, 67, 75–76, 85, 90
beings, cultural, 130
beliefs, 6, 14, 19–20, 31, 100–101, 103–4, 142
  cultural, 100
believers, 13, 28, 81–82, 89, 92, 110, 127, 134
  early church, 107
Berkowitz, Peter, 9, 141
Bernstein, Basil, 45–46.141
Berryman, 44, 47–48, 141
Bettez, Silvia C, 59–60, 141, 144

Index

Bible iv, 23–24, 27, 32, 57, 67–68, 73, 75, 77–78, 81, 85, 88, 96, 102, 106, 108–9, 115, 142, 145–47
Biblical basis, 19, 58, 95, 142
Biblical Foundations v, 15, 19, 40, 59, 61, 66–67, 69, 71, 73, 75, 77, 79, 81, 85, 87, 89, 91, 93–95, 97
Biblical Foundations for Multiculturalism v, 15, 66–67, 69, 71, 94
Biblical Foundations for social justice, 59, 61
Biblical idea of Justice, 58, 143
Biblical Justice, 58, 63, 145
biculturalism, 104
bless, 9, 72, 75, 77, 79, 86, 88, 107, 132
blessing, 9, 72, 77, 86–87, 107, 117
blind, 14, 25, 64, 88, 106, 109, 151
blood, 68, 75, 79 –, 80, 92–93, 140, 144
Bloomington, 123, 126
Bode, 108–9, 118, 146
body of christ
books, 17–18, 23, 51–53, 61, 120, 122, 142, 144–45
boundaries, cultural, 101
Bourdieu, Pierre, 45, 141
Boutte, Gloria, 105, 141
Bowles, Samuel, 44–45, 142
BP (British Petroleum), 129
Brethren church, 23
brothers, 82, 98, 122
Burnett vi, 68–69, 71, 142

California viii, 23, 52, 58, 137, 147
Canaan, 77–78, 87
Canaanites, 32, 79
Canada, 19
Cappadocia, 81–82
Cardoza-Orlandi, 112, 114, 142
catholics, roman, 6–7
change, 7, 12, 18, 22, 26, 35–38, 41–43, 48, 58, 102, 105–6, 110, 118–20, 129, 137–38, 140
transformational, 26
charity, 58
Chege, Mwangi, 142
child, 9, 31, 50, 56, 83, 99, 125
children, 19, 46, 50–51, 53–55, 70–71, 79, 101, 110, 122, 126, 134, 139

Choice (s), 19, 32, 77078, 86, 108, 110, 118, 137, 146
Christ viii, 22, 29–30, 39, 48, 63–65, 68, 70–71, 73, 81–83, 88–89, 91–93, 95, 97, 101, 107–10, 114, 123, 125–26, 130, 133–35, 140
Christ, Jesus, 19, 21, 25, 48, 82–83, 95, 101, 109, 123, 126, 130, 133
Christian iii. iv. v. vii-viii, 1–4, 10, 13–19, 22–25, 27–35, 39–40, 47–48, 50–51, 57, 61, 68, 73, 79, 92, 94, 97–98, 101, 113, 116–19.121, 123–24, 126, 133, 136–40, 142–47
circles, 31, 57
  community, iii. iv. vii-viii, 1, 4, 16, 29, 31, 123, 136–40
  doctrines, 14, 113
  education, 30, 117, 145–46
  faith, 4, 10, 14, 17, 29, 47
  higher education, 98, 145–47
  idea, 94
  leader, 18
  perspective, 24, 31, 44
  principles, 40, 61
  responses vii, 2, 15–16
  teachers, 116–19
  values , 4, 31
  voices, 16, 23
  worldview, v, 1, 16, 19, 31, 56
Christianity, 2–4, 17–18, 22–24, 27–28, 37, 39, 48, 108, 142, 144–45
Christians, 1, 3–7, 13–14, 21–22, 27–28, 32, 39, 47–48, 50, 56–57, 68, 78, 93, 99–100, 108–9, 111, 113, 124–26
church
  american, 90–91, 130–131
  asian, 131
  chinese, 31, 130
  christian vii-viii, 73
  christocentric, 133
  corinthian, 134
  early, 74, 127
  ethnic, 81
  evangelical, 14, 27, 68, 129
  first-century, v, viii, 15, 89, 128–33, 135
  homogenous, 130
  infant, 88

Index

institutional, 21
large, 124, 136
local, 134
twenty-first century, v, viii, 15, 128–33, 135
unitarian, 4
urban, 131
white, 131
church-based solutions, 9
Church Diversity, 133, 147
church structures, 93
citizens, 9, 51, 60–63, 101, 104, 116, 119, 141
class struggles, 36
classroom, 45–46, 54, 110, 114, 116–18, 143
colleges, 137–38
Colson, Charles, 16, 18–19, 142
columbus, 51, 144
comfort zones, 25–26, 56
command, 20, 25, 61, 80–81, 85, 97–98, 101, 106–7
commitment, 60–61, 79, 108, 123, 130, 132–33, 139
community, 43, 60, 71, 81
　christ-confessing, 83
　covenant, 82
　cultural , 104
　evangelical, 2
　global, 130
　human, 48
　lgbt, 30
　multicultural, 134, 136, 139–40
　new, 92
　of faith viii
　of shalom, 46, 98–99, 102, 112–14, 117–18, 130, 135, 145
　peaceful, 106
　perfect, , 112
　shalom, v-vi, 96, 98–99, 121, 123
competencies, cross-cultural, 107
conditions, socio-cultural, 44
conflict, 14, 16–17.19, 28–29, 31, 44, 102, 113, 117, 142
conscientization, 43
consciousness, cultural, 104
conservatism, 5–11, 13, 26, 141, 143–44
conservatives, 6–10, 12–14, 146

crunchy, 7
social, 7–8
constitutional
cultural, 7
fiscal, 8
contemporary thought, 16–17, 19, 21, 23, 25, 27, 29, 31, 33
content integration, 51–53, 56
contexts
　cross-cultural, 44, 100
　cultural, 104
　multicultural, 25, 71, 145
contextualized education, 114–17, 120
Contextualized Gospel, 130, 132
contextualized pedagogy, 99, 101, 114, 116
contributions, ix, 51, 53, 130
control, 9–10, 12, 14, 34–35, 39–40, 45–46, 58, 141
corporations, 128–29
covenant viii, 62–63, 66, 73–83, 85–88, 94
　new, 78, 82–83
　relationship viii, 75–79, 82–83, 87, 94
creation, 19–21, 32, 38, 48, 61, 66, 70, 74, 76, 84, 92, 94, 96, 102, 107–8, 111, 113, 129, 147
creator, 58–59, 84, 87, 97, 123
critical pedagogists, 41
critical pedagogy, 34, 41–43, 142–43, 145, 147
cross-cultural competence, 99–101, 104, 106–7, 130–131
cross-cultural conflict, 102, 142
Cross-Cultural Language and Academic Development (CLAD), 116, 142
cross cultural perspective, 23, 141, 144
cross-cultural witnesses, 107
Culture (s), 7, 17, 20–32, 34–35, 39–40, 44, 46, 51, 53, 55–56, 62–63, 71–72, 89, 93, 96–97, 100–103, 105–6, 110–112, 114–17, 120, 122, 124, 126, 129, 131, 134–35, 140–146
cultural absolutes, 40
　absolutism, 46
　bigotry, 131
　capital, 45, 141

151

Index

competence, 100–101, 104–6, 111, 131, 142
competency, 101, 107, 136
diversity, vii-viii, 20, 25, 46, 71, 102, 116, 120, 141
evolution, 12, 24
groups, 24, 31, 35, 46, 104
heritage, 26, 103, 116
identity, vi, 72, 91, 99–100, 102–4, 130, 136, 143–44
identity clarification, 104
imperialism, 109
incompetence, 100
lenses, 129
mandate, 20, 25, 85
movements, 38
parity, 54
racism, 53
relativism, 46, 97
reproduction theory, 44–46
traits, 71
transformation, 25–26
validity, 24
values, 97, 104, 106, 117
values adjustment, 106
curriculum, 40, 45, 50–51, 53, 55–56, 97, 105, 118, 20, 141
curses, 77, 86, 88, 107

David, 61–62, 68, 142, 144–46
death, 2, 21, 69, 75, 90, 92, 124–26
decodification, 115–16
dehumanization, 63
departure, 2, 78, 134
descendants, 72–73, 75–78, 81, 87, 107
destiny, 2, 59, 72, 78–79, 87, 90, 144, 146
destroy, 3, 62, 71, 75–76, 83, 99, 123
Diaz-Rico, 116, 142
differences, 5, 17, 19, 24, 30, 35–36, 40, 42, 53, 55, 68, 95, 101, 103, 06, 118, 129–31, 134–35, 144
  cultural, 19, 24, 106, 129, 135, 144
  worldview, 131
dignity, 4–5, 58, 70, 90, 109–10, 121, 123
disciples, 85–88, 101, 107–8, 131
Discipleship, 85–88

discourse, 35, 41–42, 50, 125, 143
discrimination, 10, 63–64, 106, 118, 123
dispensation, new, 88–89
dispersion, 72, 74
distortions, 21–22, 84
diversity vii-viii, 7–8, 16, 20, 25, 30–32, 40, 46, 51, 53, 55, 66–67, 71–72, 89–90, 102, 104–7, 109–10, 116, 118, 120, 125, 127, 130–131, 133–35, 137, 139–40, 146–47
DomNwachukwu viii-iv, 36, 106, 142
dynamics, 1, 20, 44, 106, 114

earth, 2–3, 20–21, 28–29, 53, 64–67, 71–77, 79, 83–87, 89–90, 92–93, 99, 107–9, 125, 134
Eden, 31–32, 59, 73, 84, 88
education v. vii-viii, 15, 17, 30–31, 35–36, 38–48, 50–51, 53–56, 59–60, 96–99, 101–2, 104–5, 107, 110–112, 114–20, 126, 137, 141–47
  contextualized, 114–17, 120
  culturally-informed, 115–16, 146
  teacher, 119, 141, 143, 145
  multicultural, 53–56, 99, 102, 104, 107, 110–112, 114–15, 117–20
  public, 101
educators vi, 16, 34–36, 40–41, 46, 114, 116–17, 120, 142–43
Edwards, Chuck, 2, 142
Edwards, Jonathan, 7
Egypt, 61, 80–81, 108, 132
election, 78, 80–82, 86–87, 93
engagement vii, 1, 16, 27, 104, 110, 119, 125, 143
Enlightenment, vi, 3, 37–38, 146
enterprise, global, 129
epistle, 82
equality, 5–6, 9, 12, 45, 48–49, 55, 60, 90, 94, 97, 111–12, 118
equity, 15, 51, 54–56, 97–98, 110, 118, 132
  ideals of, 110, 118
  pedagogy, 15, 51, 54, 56
Erickson, Millard J, 112–13, 142
establishment, 11, 61, 91
ethnic groups, 97, 104, 110, 119–20
ethnicities, 5, 31, 105, 107

Index

European cultures, 53
Europeans, 51
evangelicals, 68
evangelism, 27-29, 141
evil, 21, 24, 62-63, 65, 70, 73, 124-25, 142
experiences, 28, 43-44, 46, 51-52, 54, 100, 115-17, 121-22, 131, 141
   cultural, 44, 100

faculties, 59
fairness, 58, 60, 65, 97, 109-10, 118, 130, 133
faith viii, 3-5, 7, 10, 13-14, 17-19, 23, 28-29, 36, 38, 42, 47-48, 58, 64-65, 80, 82-83, 86-87, 93, 95, 100, 123-26, 133, 135, 137, 140, 142, 145
Fallacies v. vii, 34-35
families, 45, 87, 122, 126
fatherless, 132
fathers, founding, 90
features, 67-68, 102-3, 113
   biological, 103
   cultural, 102-3
fellowship viii, 1, 70, 73, 84, 91-92, 108
Ferm, Deane Willa, 44, 47, 143
Fiscal Conservatives, 6-8
fish, 32, 66, 75-76, 84
flesh, 67
flood, 75-76
framework, 5, 19-20, 41, 75, 97, 105, 117, 146
freedom, 5, 9-10, 41, 44, 52, 57, 59, 64-65, 70, 90, 109, 143
   individual, 9, 90
   religious, 9-10
Freire, Paulo, 41, 43-44, 48, 114-16, 119-20, 143,
Frey, Christopher, 58, 143
fulfillment, 88-90, 97, 117, 145

Galileo, 3
garden, 31, 32, 84, 85, 107
Gardner, Howard, 60, 61, 143
gender, 32, 35, 47, 48, 55, 67, 103, 114, 118, 146

generations, 11, 36, 44, 51, 63, 76, 82, 87, 98
Genesis, 66-68, 71, 74, 79, 84, 98, 107-8, 112, 145
Gentiles, 82, 88-90, 107, 126
Gi, Jie, 34, 35, 36, 40, 143
Gintis, Herbart, 44, 45, 142
Giroux, Henry, 42, 44, 119, 143, 145
Glasser, Arthur, 67, 71-75, 78, 81-83, 85, 89, 91, 143
Global World, 141
globalization, 8, 128, 129
goal of multicultural education, 15, 37, 46, 50-56, 97, 99, 112, 117-18
God of justice, 20, 58, 61-65, 74, 94
Goodhart, R. Lee, 5, 53, 55, 144
Gorski, Paul, 110, 119, 143
gospel
   of Christ, 30, 65, 89
government
   action, 6
   involvement (regulation), 9, 10, 12
grace
   of God, 70, 125
Grant, Carl, 110, 118, 146
Greco-Roman culture, 31
group (s)
   conservative Christian, 4, 50
   cultural/racial, 103

Haddad, Daphne, 46, 143
Haidt, Jonathan, 14, 144
Handbook of Research on Multicultural Education, 55, 141, 145
harmony, 98
hate (hate crime), 6, 108, 123-26
heart of God, 61, 63, 65, 85
heavens, 3, 72, 89
Hernandez, Hilda, 110, 118
Hesselgrave, David, 23, 48, 144
Hindus, 13-14
Hispanic churches, 131
historical enlightenment paradigm, 37-38
holiness, 29
holy spirit, 21, 71, 75, 81, 83, 88, 100, 101, 131

Index

homogeneity, cultural, 100
Horenczyk, Gabriel, 102, 103, 143
Hubbard, David, 78, 80, 84, 87,
Human (s)
  diversity, 66, 71, 72
  history, 25, 34, 72, 74, 75, 83, 88
  knowledge, 3, 72
  life, 20, 114
  race, 32, 67-68, 71, 73-74, 77, 113
  universals, 103
humanism, 2-4
humanistic philosophers, 3-4
humankind, 3, 21, 32, 66-67, 69, 112
Hytten, Kathy, 59, 60

idea of multiculturalism, 1, 2, 31, 35, 50, 57, 63, 120
ideals
  liberal, 12
  lofty conservatism, 10
identity
  christ-centered, 130, 133
ideologies
  marxist, 34-37, 40, 94, 142
  postmodern, 34-40, 42, 46
image
  of God, 58, 66-68, 75, 85, 94, 99, 107, 110, 129
Imago Dei, 66, 69-70, 99
immersion
  cultural, 29
immigration, 8, 102, 123
immortality, 69
inclusiveness, 37, 40, 83
individual liberty, 6-7
individual right, 9, 10, 60
individual differences, 17
inequalities
  social, 111, 118
injustices
  personal, 61
  racial, 57
  social, 62
institutionalized discrimination, 63
institutions
  cultural, 29
  educational, 35, 101, 118, 119
intentional intervention, 111, 118

interaction
  cultural, 105
intercultural communication, 23

Japanese culture, 129
Jesus
  Christ, 19, 21, 25, 48, 82, 95, 101
  Jesus's teaching, 114-15, 145
John Wilson Wallace, 121-23
Joldersma, Clarence, 144
judgment, 25, 74, 108
justice
  defining, 20, 41, 58-59, 118
  social, 59-61
  Biblical, 61-65

kingdom
  motif, 112-20
  of God, 71, 89, 92-94
klesis, 92
Knight, George, 38-39, 41
knowledge
  construction, 51, 53-54
koinonia, 91-92
Koppelman, Kent, 53, 55, 144
Korean church, 123-27
Kowalski, Charles, 103, 144
Kraft, Charles, 16, 23-26, 144

Ladson-Billings, 114, 120, 145
Land
  of Canaan, 77-78, 87
Language, 7, 13, 27, 35, 38-39, 51, 55, 71, 100-101
Latin America, 43, 47, 132
Laws
  creational, 20
  of nature, 20
Learning
  Cultural, 106
  Environment, 110, 118-19
  Styles, 45, 106
Lee, H, 114-15, 145
Liberal Beliefs, 6
Liberalism, 11-12
Liberals, 6, 12, 14
Liberation, 42-43, 57, 64
Liberation theology, 34, 47-49, 94

Index

Libertarians, 8, 10, 12
Liberty
  individual, 6
  personal, 10, 12
Life
  Christ-centric vs. communitarian, 92
lifestyles, 7, 27, 30, 32, 93, 121
Lingenfelter, Judith & Sherwood, 115, 145
literacy and Hegemony, 41, 142
Love of God, 20, 97, 114, 121, 125

Macchia, F. D, 89, 145
Manifest destiny, 78, 79, 87, 90, 144
mankind, 4, 20, 32, 61, 66–67, 71, 73, 75–78, 84–85, 112
marginalization, 7, 63, 109
markets, free, 8, 133
Marshall, Chris, 58, 63, 145
Marxism (Marxist), 18–19, 34–37, 40
Mcclay, Wilfred, 11, 145
McGavran, Donald, 23, 145
Mclaren, Peter, 119, 143, 145
melting pot, 17, 25
membership, 45, 93, 103
ministry (cross-cultural), 107–8
minorities, suppressed history of, 30
Mission of God, 84–91
missionaries, 23, 25
models
  counter-system, 93
modernism (modernity), 38–39
moral quality, 58–59
Moses (Law of), 61, 80, 93, 108, 132
multicultural education
  as content integration, 51–53
  as knowledge construction, 53–54
  as equity pedagogy, 54–55
  as prejudice reduction, 55
  as empowering a new school culture, 55–56
  radical, 46–47
multiculturalism
  biblical foundation, 66–95
  Christian view, 34–49
multicultural church, 81, 134–35
multicultural community
  community, 134
  steps, 136–40
multicultural competencies, 106
multicultural contexts, 25, 71, 96
multicultural education
  objectives, 104
  strategies, 54, 101, 114, 120
multicultural educators, 35, 40, 119–20
multicultural
  ideas, 31
  ideology, 17
  model, 99
  organization, 134
  principles, 40
  schools, 53
  society, 100
  stories, 121–27

Nardoni, Enrique, 64, 145
nationality, 64, 103, 134
nationhood, 87
nations (holy), 80, 82, 93, 131
Native American church, 130
natural world, 4, 72
Negro Race in America, 52, 147
Neoconservatives, 6, 8, 11
new covenant, 78, 82–83
New paradigm of multiculturalism, 96–111
Newton, Jon, 30–31, 40, 146
Ng, David, 146
Niebuhr, Reinhold, 16, 22–23, 72, 146
Nieto, Sonja, 41, 108, 109, 118, 146
Noah, 66, 72–94
Noahic covenant, 76
Noebel, David, 2, 146
non-Christian community (world), 28
norms, 20–21
North America, 90

obedience, 23, 77, 80, 85, 93
objectified capital, 45
objective
  reality, 38
  truths, 38, 39
oppression
  social, 41, 109
  history of, 97
  five faces of, 109

Index

ordinances of God, 21
O'sullivan, John, 90, 91, 144
outreach (intentional), 134, 139
Ozele, Anthony, 115, 116, 146

Paleoconservatives, 7, 8
Palmer, Parker, 113, 146
Panikulam, George, 91, 146
participation
   Critical, 27–28
   Cultural, 29
Paul, 126, 130, 134
Pauline theology, 91–92
peace, 32, 63, 65, 83, 90, 97, 107, 112, 122, 125, 134
Pearcey, Nancy, 1, 16, 18, 19, 142
peasants, 43–44, 116
pedagogy of the oppressed, 41, 43, 114, 120, 143
Pentecost, 81, 88–91, 100, 134
plan
   of God, 73–74, 82, 86, 88, 90, 100, 137
pluralism (plurality)
   cultural, 40, 46
political
   correctness, 18–19, 133
   ideologies, 2, 4–6, 10, 13–14, 123
populists, 12, 41
Postmodern World/idea, 16, 31–32, 42
postmodernism (postmodernity), 30
   multiculturalism as postmodernism, 37–40
poverty, 8, 9, 47–48
power (political), 34–35, 42–44
praxis
   pedagogy of, 41, 43–44
   praxis for contextualized education, 114–17
   praxis for social justice, 117–20
prejudice
   reduction, 51, 55, 70, 72, 88, 108, 118
preservation of ecosystem, 76
privileges
   cultural, 77
process
   of Cultural Transformation, 23, 26
proletariat, 18, 35–36

prophecy, 85
Protagoras, 2, 3

Quinn, Justin, 7, 8, 146

racial superiority, 78, 79
racism, 47, 53, 78–79, 106
reconciliation, 113, 125
reform process, 15, 31, 35, 119
Reformation
   of Culture, 21
Reformational Worldview, 19
Reich, Robert, 45, 146
rejectionists, 27–28
relationship (s)
   i-Thou, 79–82
   personal, 77–79, 82, 83, 87, 94
reproduction theory, 41, 44–46
responsibilities (individual), 60
restoration, 8, 21, 31–32
righteousness, 13, 18, 32, 61–62, 77, 83, 85, 117, 135
rights
   human, 6, 42
   individual, 9, 10, 60
Romans, 20, 130

salvation, 18, 39, 81, 91–92, 100, 130
sanctification, 21–22
school
   culture, 55, 56, 114, 120
   curriculum, 55
   systems, 35, 44–45, 54, 101
schooling, 34–35, 41, 44–45, 54, 110, 119
Schooling in Capitalist America
schools
   home, 50, 101
   parochial, 101
   public, 50, 101
   transformation of, 110, 119
secular
   Humanism, 2–4
segregation (separation), cultural, 112
   Social, 27, 100
   Racial, 70
shalom
   community of, 112–14, 130, 135

model, 97, 102
motif, 96, 111, 123
sin (human), 21, 28–29, 32, 71–73, 85, 97, 110
situations
  cross-cultural, 100
skills
  cross-cultural, 105
Sleeter, Christine, 110, 118, 146
Snyder, Howard, 93, 94, 147
social
  change, 22, 42, 118–20
  justice, 41, 57–65, 130, 132–33
society
  capitalistic, 44–47
  classless, 36
  ideal, 11
  transformation of, 110, 119–20
  unequal, 7, 41
sociopolitical context of multicultural, 150
Sproul, R. C, 3, 4, 16, 17, 28, 147
standards, cultural, 29
Standish, Paul, 60, 147
Steinberg, Shirley, 42, 147
strangers, 79, 82, 113
strategies (teaching), 54, 101, 105, 114, 120
structures (social/cultural), 26, 29, 30, 34, 36, 41, 51, 102
subcultures, 26
superstructure, 34
symbols, 35, 115, 117
system
  social/cultural, 17, 44, 100
  school, 44, 45, 53–55, 97, 101, 110

teachers (educators), 16, 30, 40, 42–43, 54, 56, 106, 114–17
teaching
  effective cross-cultural, 114–17
tolerance, 7, 11, 17, 30–31, 40, 55, 105, 112

Toope, Deborah, 60, 61
transformative intellectuals, 119

unchristian, 48, 70
unity (and diversity), 67, 68, 71–74, 89, 93
universe, 37, 60, 85, 102, 112
unpatriotic, 41

vacuum, cultural, 100
validity, cultural, 24, 38, 101
values
  cultural, 97, 104, 106, 117
  traditional American, 6–7

Weed, Katherine, 116, 142
Western culture, 24–26
wholeness, 29, 97, 112
Williams, Scott, 133, 147
willingness
Willis, Richard, 70, 147
Wolters, Albert, 16, 19–22, 96, 102, 147
Wolterstorff, Nicholas, 44, 98, 147
world
  fallen, 98, 113, 121
  globalized, 111
worldviews
  premodern vs. modern vs. postmodern, 38
  modern, 38
  contemporary Christian worldview, 1–15
  multiculturalism worldview, 16–33
  secular humanistic, 2

Yahweh, 62, 63, 81, 82
Yoder, Perry, 97, 98, 147

Zinn, Howard, 52

www.ingramcontent.com/pod-product-compliance
Lightning Source LLC
Chambersburg PA
CBHW051105160426
43193CB00010B/1323